THE MARTYRDOM OF LOVEJOY

THE MARTYRDOM OF LOVEJOY

AN ACCOUNT

OF THE

LIFE, TRIALS AND PERILS

OF

REV. ELIJAH P. LOVEJOY

WHO WAS KILLED BY A PRO-SLAVERY MOB

AT ALTON, ILLINOIS, THE NIGHT OF NOVEMBER 7, 1837

BY AN EYE-WITNESS

[HENRY TANNER]

[1881]

AUGUSTUS M. KELLEY · PUBLISHERS

NEW YORK 1971

First Edition 1881

(Chicago: Fergus Printing Company, 1881)

REPRINTED 1971 BY
AUGUSTUS M. KELLEY • PUBLISHERS
REPRINTS OF ECONOMIC CLASSICS
New York New York 10001

. . . .

I S B N 0 - 6 7 8 - 0 0 7 4 4 - 6
L C N 68 - 18603

. . . .

PRINTED IN THE UNITED STATES OF AMERICA
by SENTRY PRESS, NEW YORK, N. Y. 10019

!! Look at This !!

: Coffins Coffins :

50 Ready made "Walnut Coffins on hand and some for sale by The subscriber

James Mansfield

Apply To old Royal's Alton

This is the fac-simile of an original order issued to the Captain of one squad of men in the building at the time the press was received, and the mob expected to attack it, if at all,—and was the night before the killing of Lovejoy.

THE MARTYRDOM OF LOVEJOY.

THE MARTYRDOM OF LOVEJOY.

AN ACCOUNT

OF THE

LIFE, TRIALS, AND PERILS

OF REV.

ELIJAH P. LOVEJOY

WHO WAS

KILLED BY A PRO-SLAVERY MOB,

AT

ALTON, ILL., ON THE NIGHT OF NOVEMBER 7, 1837.

BY AN EYE-WITNESS.

If I, my lord, for my opinion bleed,
Opinion shall be surgeon to my hurt,
And keep me on the side where still I am.
HENRY VI, Act 2, Scene 4.

CHICAGO:
FERGUS PRINTING COMPANY,
1881.

INTRODUCTION.

IT has seemed desirable, to many of my friends, that I, who was somewhat intimately associated with the Christian patriot who edited the *St. Louis Observer* and the *Alton Observer*, in the early days of the anti-slavery contest, should put on record, in a connected form, details of which I happened to become personally cognizant—matters of history relating to the death of Elijah P. Lovejoy, which, unless recorded *now* by one who knew the facts, would be lost sight of forever. This has seemed, to my friends, the more important because no single event in the early history of the progress of the anti-slavery sentiment in the United States produced a more profound impression, at the time, than the successive destruction, by mobs, of the *four* print-ing-presses which belonged to Mr. Lovejoy, and in the defence of the last of which, under the sanction of civil authority, he sacrificed his life.

In compiling, I am in debt to the memoir of Lovejoy, by his brothers, Joseph and Owen, to Wm. S. Lincoln's notes of trials of the defenders of the press, and to other publications of that day, long since out of print and now scarcely ever met with. My own remembrance of the scenes, in most of which I was an actor, has also been refreshed by conversations with Col. George T. M. Davis and Winthrop S. Gilman, of New York City, who were residents of Alton at that time, and with A. W. Corey, of Godfrey, Illinois, Abram Breath, and the late Lawson A. Parks, both of the City of Alton.

Another object I have in mind in presenting these records to the public is, to vindicate the memory of Lovejoy from an absurd charge, made by some, that he broke his pledge in discussing the subject of slavery in the columns of the *Alton Observer*. And lastly, it is my wish to bear testimony to the meek and noble Christian character which marked this estimable man, who, with all the firmness of the early Christian martyrs, faced enemies frenzied with passion, who would have stopped at nothing to compass his ruin.

PREFACE.

---

*"The popular knowledge of history, which is none the less important because specialists may think that it can not but be superficial, must always be imparted by means of personal narrative.   *   *   *   *   The mass of mankind, who have little leisure for reading, and no motive for it but amusement, will not read any more about States and Governments than can be presented to them in biographies of famous men."*—J. R. SEELEY, M.A.

THE key to the present is found in the past, and the American citizen who would know how to meet the political questions, which are constantly arising in our affairs, must be well-grounded in the history of the successive steps by which the present condition of parties and issues in this country has been reached.

The march of events during the past forty years has been very rapid, and, while the latest great struggle has passed into history, it is still sufficiently vivid to most adults to dim the recollection of the events that preceded it, which, as germs of that great uprising, are of the utmost importance.

The narrative related in the following pages is an un-varnished tale of the shedding of the first blood in defence of the liberty of the press, at the beginning of the discussion of the subject of negro slavery in the United States.

Elijah Parish Lovejoy, a Presbyterian minister, editor of a religious newspaper, was attacked by a mob and killed, at Alton, Illinois, on the night of 7th November, 1837. During a comparatively brief period, three of his printing-presses had been successively destroyed by mobs, and it was when engaged, with the sanction of the civil authority in the defence of a fourth, that he gave up his life.

The martyrdom of Lovejoy had a most important influence in setting forward public sentiment in favor of the liberties of the people and of obedience to constitutional law. It seems, therefore, to be worthy of careful re-examination and thoughtful consideration at this time.

It is difficult for the present generation to realize the intensity of the excitement that was produced forty years ago by the death of this brave man, and the previous events which it emphasized. He died a martyr to the cause of the freedom of the press, for which John Milton so eloquently pleaded in his "Areopagitica," at a time when that freedom was violently assailed—he died a champion of constitutional law, when that law was openly defied through the length and breadth of the land, and no single event in the early history of the anti-slavery struggle produced a more profound impression throughout the country.*

---

* The extent and depth of the feeling aroused at the time will be made clear by the following brief extracts. William Ellery Channing, D.D., used this language, in an address to his fellow-citizens, of Boston:

"An event has occurred which ought to thrill the hearts of this people as the heart of one man. A martyr has fallen among us to the freedom of the press. A citizen has been murdered in defence of the right of free discussion. I do not ask whether he was christian or unbeliever, whether he was abolitionist or colonizationist. He has been murdered in exercising what I hold to be

It is proper for me to state that I was an actor in many of the scenes described, was—in company with other gentlemen—with Mr. Lovejoy in the warehouse where his fourth press was stored at the time of its defence, and by his side when he died. I have taken advantage of the reminiscenses of personal friends, some of whom have largely aided me in this work, and have extracted freely from a Memoir of Lovejoy, by his brothers (1838), from Lincoln's notes of trials of the defenders of the press, from Wendell Phillips' speeches, and from other publications, some of which have been long out of print and are not easily accessible.

I am indebted to Winthrop S. Gilman, Esq., of New York, one of the original twenty defenders, and owner of the building where the press was stored; and to his son, Arthur Gilman, M.A., of Cambridge, Mass., for valuable service in arranging the contents of this work, and preparing it for the press.

                                        HENRY TANNER,
BUFFALO, N.Y., 1880.

---

the dearest right of the citizen. Nor is this a solitary act of violence. It is the consummation of a long series of assaults on public order, on freedom, on the majesty of the laws."

Of this brief period of history John Quincy Adams wrote as follows:

"The incidents which preceded and accompanied and followed the catastrophy of Mr. Lovejoy's death, point it out as an epoch in the annals of human liberty. They have given a shock as of an earthquake throughout this continent."

The *Boston Recorder* manifested the excitement produced when the editor declared that the events called forth from every part of the land "A burst of indignation which has not had its parallel in this country since the battle of Lexington, in 1775."

CONTENTS.

CHAPTER XVII.

CHAPTER XVIII.

CHAPTER XIX.

CHAPTER XX.

CHAPTER XXI.

CHAPTER XXII.

CHAPTER XXIII.

APPENDIX.

APPENDIX B.

APPENDIX C.

THE MARTYRDOM OF LOVEJOY.

CHAPTER I.

The Times—Excitement on the subject of Slavery—Determined
spirit of the opposing parties.

THE early period of the anti-slavery movement, is well
known to have been one of intense excitement, and of
vehement action. Slavery was becoming the question of
the generation. On the one side was* a money-power of
two-thousand millions of dollars, as the prices of slaves
then ranged, held by a small body of able and desperate
men, who composed a political aristocracy by special constitutional provisions; with cotton, the product of slave-
labor, forming the basis of our whole foreign commerce,
and with the heart of the common people chilled by a
bitter prejudice against the black race. On the same side
was the pecuniary interest of the Northern people, who
found in the Southern States the most profitable purchasers
for all their products. On the other side, a comparatively
small number of hated abolitionists, whose sole capital was
their ideas, and whose sole supporters were the men who
insisted on free speech, a free press, and obedience to constitutional law.

* See speeches of Wendell Phillips.

In such a contest, they who from principle attacked slavery, did so at the peril of their lives, each realizing that he might be called "to die for the people, that the whole nation perish not."

William Lloyd Garrison, a man justly honored since his death, thus opposed it with great spirit and severity of language. He was mobbed in Massachusetts, and put in prison, at the very cradle of liberty, for his free utterances; nad, in return, he boldly and eloquently proclaimed: "Is there not cause for severity? I will be as harsh as truth, and as uncompromising as justice. I am in earnest—I will not equivocate—I will not excuse—I will not retreat a single inch—and I will be heard."

A mob surged through the streets of Boston in 1835, at the time when the Mayor of that city broke up a public meeting of a "Female Anti-Slavery Society." Said the Mayor: "Go home ladies, go home. Don't stop ladies, go home. Indeed, ladies, you must retire, it is dangerous to remain." The ladies believed they had rights, and one of them fearlessly replied in the spirit of '76: "If this is the last bulwark of freedom, we may as well die here." Nevertheless, they did retire in an orderly manner, and completed their meeting at a private house. Mr. Francis Jackson, in answering a letter of thanks for the use of his house, gave expression to the common determination of those who would not surrender their rights, in this notable language. "If a large majority of this community choose to turn a deaf ear to the wrongs which are inflicted on their countrymen in other portions of the land—if they are content to turn away from the sight of oppression, and pass by on the other side—so it must be. But when they undertake in any way to impair or annul my right to speak, write, and publish upon any subject—and more especially upon enormities, which are the common concern of every lover of his country, and his kind—so it must *not* be—so it shall not be, if I, for one, can prevent it. Upon this great right let us hold on at all hazards. And should we, in its exercise, be driven from public halls to private dwellings, one house at least shall be consecrated to its preservation. And if, in defence of this sacred privilege, which man did not give me, and shall not (if I can help it) take from me, this roof, and these walls, shall be levelled to the earth—let them fall, if they must. They can not crumble in a better cause. They will appear of very little value to me, after their owner shall have been whipped into silence."

The opposition among slaveholders, and their allies, and their determination to silence free discussion, legally if they could, but forcibly if they must, were quite as great and positive as was the earnestness of Mr. Jackson, Mr. Garrison, and the friends of order, who scouted the idea of surrendering the liberty of speaking and publishing what they pleased on the subject of slavery.

Southern legislatures were ready to dissolve the Union—passed stringent laws against enlightening slaves, and Southern gentlemen did not consider it beneath their dignity to hunt and whip men who were even suspected of Abolitionism.

Northern States were called on to silence the discussion of the dreaded subject. The mails were rifled in order to prevent the introduction of Abolition publications in the South.

The right of petitioning the government to abolish slavery in the District of Columbia was denied; and no man traveling in the South, who was supposed to favor Abolitionism, was safe, either in person or property. Ministers, who publicly prayed for the slave, were often looked upon with a threatening eye.

At the time of this excitement, and between the fire of this array of opposing parties—each of whom preferred to die than to yield—Mr. Lovejoy was publishing a religious newspaper, on the banks of the Mississippi, in 1835–1837. He believed it to be his duty to stand firmly in full sympathy with the defenders of free speech—if need be to suffer with them—and between their principles and those of slaveholders a compromise was, in the nature of things, a moral impossibility.

Mr. Lovejoy's paper, the *St. Louis Observer*, afterwards the *Alton Observer*, was the organ of zealous Presbyterians and Congregationalists in Illinois and Missouri, who insisted that it was his duty—as he himself fully believed—to die at his editorial post, if need be, rather than surrender the right of free speech and a free press.

CHAPTER II.

Lovejoy's Early Life.

Elijah Parish Lovejoy was born in Albion, Maine, Nov. 8, 1802. He would have been thirty-five years old the day after he was murdered. He was the son of Rev. Daniel Lovejoy, a Congregational minister, and had graduated at Waterville College, Maine. The tide of emigration was setting strongly Westward in the days of Mr. Lovejoy's early manhood, and he drifted with it to St. Louis, where he first became a school-teacher, and subsequently editor of the *St. Louis Times*, a whig newspaper. In 1832, the whole current of his life was changed by means of a remarkable conversion to the Christian faith. He ever after felt that "The disciple is not above his master, nor the servant above his lord;" and nothing could satisfy his fervent spirit, but preaching that cross which had shed such a flood of new light into his soul. He, therefore, soon entered Princeton Theological Seminary, where he progressed so rapidly that in the subsequent year, 1833, he was licensed to preach the gospel. He returned the same season to St. Louis, and, being known as a ready writer, was put in charge of the *St. Louis Observer*, then, as has been stated, the organ of Presbyterians in the States of Illinois and Missouri.

It is worthy of notice, how soon after his conversion to Christ, this mighty man, in the first flush of divine love, and with a consecration and singleness of purpose quite remarkable, was chosen to edit a leading religious newspaper. Converted in 1832, he became a minister of the gospel in 1833, and was in charge of influential editorial columns on the eleventh of November, of the latter year. He seemed to hear the voice of the spirit saying unto him: "What I tell you in darkness, that speak ye in light; and what ye hear in the ear, that preach ye upon the housetops. And fear not them which kill the body." There probably had not lived in this century a man of greater singleness of purpose in bearing witness to the truth, or one who was more meek and peaceful; or more courageous in maintaining principle in the face of passionate opposition.

Mr. Lovejoy was of medium height, broadly built, muscular, of dark complexion, black eyes, with a certain twinkle betraying his sense of the humorous, and with a countenance expressing great kindness and sympathy.

His demeanor among friends manifested meekness and patience, which nothing short of the controlling power of the Christian religion could have produced in one possessed of a will so strong and a nature so energetic.

In tracing the facts which led at last to his death, we shall soon have occasion to notice his editorials, written upon other controverted subjects than the question of slavery, and the effect they produced.

In reading these, we shall bear in mind that the period when they were written was one of powerful religious interest. Men's minds were profoundly moved; though twas forcibly stimulated; and a pungency and directness of appeal on moral and religious subjects was common, such as does not prevail in this generation.

As a result of this religious movement in the East and West, the Rôman Catholic question assumed new prominence. Men began to discuss principles as they had not done before.

A large imigration of Congregationalists and Presbyterians was at that day rushing into Illinois and Missouri, with the avowed design of laying the foundations of new cities and villages, and of establishing colleges and other institutions in order to mould society according to the principles of the gospel. Mr. Lovejoy participated in the common-missionary feeling of ardent Christian men, and felt it his duty to hold up their hands and boldly to attack sin, irrespective of the question as to how strongly or how respectably it was intrenched. Remembering these facts, we can the better appreciate his editorials and understand his position as a writer.

A melancholy interest attaches to the following lines, selected from a few fugitive poems of Mr. Lovejoy, because they evince a vague presentiment that his life would be short, and his blood might be shed "in freedom's holiest cause":

FAREWELL TO MY NATIVE LAND.

"Land of my birth! my natal soil farewell;
The winds and waves are bearing me away
Fast from thy shores; and I would offer thee
This sincere tribute of a swelling heart.
I love thee; witness that I do, my tears,
Which gushingly do flow, and will not be restrained
At thought of seeing thee, perchance, no more.

Yes, I do love thee; though thy hills are bleak,
And piercing cold thy winds; though winter blasts
Howl long and dreary o'er thee, and thy skies
Frown oftener than they smile; though thine is not
The rich profusion that adorns the year in sunnier climes,
Though spicy-gales blow not in incense from thy groves.
For thou hast that, far more than worth them all.
Health sits upon thy rugged hills, and blooms in all thy
        vales;
Thy laws are just, or if they ever lean,
'Tis to sweet mercy's side at pity's call.
Thy sons are noble, in whose veins there runs
A richer tide than Europe's kings can boast;
The blood of freemen; blood which oft has flowed
In Freedom's holiest cause; and ready yet to flow,
If need should be, ere•it would curdle down
To the slow, sluggish stream of Slavery.
Thy daughters, too, are fair, and beauty's mien
Looks still the lovelier, graced with purity.
For these I love thee; and if these were all,
Good reason were there that thou shouldst be loved.
But other ties, and dearer far than all,
Bind fast my heart to thee.
Who can forget the scenes in which the doubtful ray
Of reason first dawned o'er him?   Can memory e'er
Forsake the home where friends, where parents dwell?
Close by the mansion where I first drew breath,
There stands a tree, beneath whose branching shade
I've sported oft in childhood's sunny hours;—
A lofty elm;—I've carved my name thereon;

There let it grow, a still increasing proof,
That time can not efface, nor distance dim
The recollection of those halcyon days.
My father, too; I've grieved his manly heart,
Full many a time, by heedless waywardness,
While he was laboring with a parent's care
To feed and clothe his thoughtless, thankless boy,
And I have trembled, as with frown severe
He oft has checked me, when perhaps I meant
To do him pleasure, with my childish mirth;
And thought how strange it was, he would not smile.
But oh! my mother! she whose every look
Was love and tenderness, that knew no check;
Who joyed with me; whose fond maternal eye
Grew dim, when pain or sorrow faded mine.
My mother! thou art thinking now of me,
And tears are thine that I have left thee so.
Oh, do not grieve, for God will hear those prayers,
Which constantly are going up to heaven,
For blessings on thy lone and wandering son.
But time is speeding, and the billow waves
Are hurrying me away. Thy misty shores
Grow dim in distance, while yon setting sun
Seems lingering fondly on them, as 'twould take,
Like me, a last adieu. I go to tread
The Western vales, whose gloomy cypress tree
Shall haply soon be wreathed upon my bier:
Land of my birth! my natal soil, Farewell."

CHAPTER III.

His religious experience—His conversion—The earnestness of
his character.

The following letters, giving to his parents an account of
his deep religious feelings, and their replies, showing the
tenderness of the family affection, throw much light upon
the martyr's character :

"ST. LOUIS, February 22, 1832.

"MY DEAR AND HONORED PARENTS:

"After reading this letter, you will, I think, be ready
to exclaim with me, 'God's ways are not our ways,
nor his thoughts as our thoughts.' When this letter
reaches you, I shall, if God spares my life and health, be
on my way to Princeton, in New Jersey, for the purpose of
entering upon my studies, preparatory to the work of the
ministry.

"I wrote you, four weeks since last Tuesday, and, as you
will have learned from that letter, was then in a state of deep
distress. Sorrow had taken hold upon me, and a sense of
my long career in sin and rebellion against God, lay heavy
upon my soul. But it pleased God, and blessed be his
holy name, to grant me, as I humbly hope, that very night,
joy and peace in believing. I was, by Divine grace, enabled to bring all my sins and all my sorrows, and lay
them at the feet of Jesus, and to receive the blessed assurance that He had accepted me, all sinful and polluted
as I was.

"My dear parents, I can see you now, after having read thus far, shedding tears of joy over the return of your prodigal son; but oh! forget not to return thanks to that God of the promises, who, as I humbly hope, has at length heard your prayers in behalf of one, for whom, at times, you were ready to say, there remaineth no longer any hope. And surely, you may well join with me in saying, that nothing but a miracle of Sovereign mercy could have arrested and saved me from eternal perdition. How I could have so long resisted the entreaties, the prayers, and the tears of my dear parents, and the influences of the Holy Spirit, is, to me, a wonder entirely incomprehensible; and still greater is my astonishment, and my admiration, that God has still borne with me, still continued unto me the influences of His spirit, and at last brought me to submit myself to Him. I think I can now have some faint conceptions of boundless, infinite mercy. I look back upon my past life, and am lost in utter amazement at the perfect folly and madness of my conduct. Why, my dear parents, it is the easiest thing in the world to become a Christian— ten thousand times easier than it is to hold out unrepenting against the motives which God presents to the mind to induce it to forsake its evil thoughts and turn unto Him. If I could forget what I have been and what I have done, I should certainly say it was impossible that any one could read of a Saviour, and not love Him with their whole heart. The eternal God—the infinite Jehovah—has done all He could do—even to the sacrificing of his own Son— to provide a way for man's happiness; and yet they reject Him, hate Him, and laugh him to scorn! How God could suffer me to live so long as I have lived, is more than I can understand. Well may He call upon the heavens to be astonished both at His own forbearance and the unnatural rebellion of His creatures. Do Christians ever feel oppressed, as it were, with the debt of gratitude which they owe to their Redeemer. Why, it seems to me, sometimes, as if I could not bear up under the weight of my obligations to God in Christ, as if they would press me to the very earth; and I am only relieved by the reflection that I have an eternity in which I may praise and magnify the riches of His grace.

"And now, my dear and honored parents, how shall I express my sense of the gratitude I owe to you—how shall I ask pardon for all the undutiful conduct of which I have been guilty towards you? I want words to do either; but I can pray to God to forgive me, and to reward you, and this I do daily. Oh, how much do I owe you for your kindness to me in every thing, but chiefly for the religious instruction you bestowed upon me from my earliest youth; for your affectionate warnings and continued entreaties that I would attend to the welfare of my own soul; and for your prayers, without ceasing, to God that He would have mercy upon me, while I had no mercy on myself. For all these, may heaven return upon your own heads a seven-fold blessing.

"I made a public profession of religion, and joined the church in this city, on the Sabbath before the last, the twelfth of the present month. With me joined also thirty-five others by profession, and four by letter. There are, probably, as many more prepared to join as soon as the next communion shall arrive. You will see by these facts, that an unusual attention to religion exists in this place. God is doing wonders here. The revival still continues, and day after to-morrow will commence a four-days' meeting. How long this state of things will continue is known only to God; but we know that he can work, and none can hinder.

"After much prayer and consultation with my pastor, Rev. William S. Potts, and other Christian friends, I have felt it my duty to turn my immediate attention to the work of the ministry, and shall, on the first of the week, start for Princeton, with a view of entering upon the necessary studies. If God shall spare my hitherto unprofitable life, I hope to be enabled to spend the remainder of it, in some measure, to His glory. Time now with me is precious, and every day seems an age, till I can be at work in the vineyard of the Lord. Oh, my dear parents, are not the ways of Providence inscrutable. How long, and how often, did you pray that your first-born son might succeed his father in preaching the gospel, and after you had, doubtless, given over all such hopes, then the Lord displays His power in calling in the wanderer.

"I hope to see you in the course of the summer, face to face; for, if practicable, and within the reach of my means, I shall take time enough in a vacation to make a visit to my dear loved home. Oh, how I long to embrace my parents, and brothers, and sisters, and tell them what God has done for me. But I feel that I ought to say, and I trust He will enable them to say, 'His will be done.' Surely, after all His goodness unto us, we should no longer indulge in one murmuring thought.

"Brother Owen, and brother John, you are now the only members of the family who have not professed to hope in Christ—to have made your peace with God. Oh, let me entreat you, beseech you, not to put it off a moment longer. Tempt not God, as I have done. Think of poor brother Daniel, and make your peace with a Saviour before you sleep, after reading this.

"Your dutiful and grateful son,

"ELIJAH P. LOVEJOY."

It may be easily imagined that the above letters gave great joy to his parents and friends. The following is the joint reply of father and mother:

"ALBION, MAINE, March 19, 1832.

"MY DEAR FIRST-BORN AND LONG ABSENT SON:

"You, perhaps, may better conceive, than I can express, the sensations your two last letters have excited in my mind.

"Your first, found me in a state of deep mental debility, to which, as you know, I have always been more or less subject. But I am now better—to which your letter has contributed much. There is no other way in which you could have given us so much joy, as you have done in the full account of your conversion, and of the intended change of your pursuits. It is just what we could have wished, had it been left to us to dictate in every particular. Let all the praise and glory be given to God through Jesus Christ. I am glad you have made haste to keep His commandments. You gave us much more credit than we think we deserve. Our faith has been wavering, and our desires far less ardent than they should have been. Our attachment to the blessed covenant has not been in proportion to its value; yet no day has passed when you have been forgotten at the throne of grace; and the blessed promises of the covenant have tended more than anything else to keep alive my hope.

"Your last letter produced sensations not unlike those, which I presume Jacob felt, when he saw the wagons sent from Egypt by his long absent son. Do not think of deferring your visit a moment longer than is absolutely necessary. Returning from Washington, I found your letter upon a generous sheet—I read and read it; and then we sang the 101st hymn, first book. We then bowed, and gave thanks to the God of heaven, who hath mercy on whom he will have mercy. Thanks to His name, that He has brought our dear son to the arms of the Saviour, and rescued him from the wrath to come. Oh, blessed be the Lord God of Abraham, and let all flesh bless His holy name. You can but know that you are greatly beloved by all the family, and no one could diffuse more happiness among us. Your mother wishes to fill the remainder.

"As ever, your affectionate father,

"DANIEL LOVEJOY."

"MY DEAR SON:

"I wrote you in answer to yours of January 22d, giving you an account of our health and circumstances. I can not say that the contents of your last letter were more than I expected; for I did really believe that God had given you a broken and contrite heart; and that is where the Holy Spirit delights to dwell. Neither can I say it is more than I have asked. It is just what I have prayed for, as I have thought, with all my heart. But I can say it is more than I deserved. But God is a Sovereign; He does not deal with us according to our deserts, nor reward us according to our iniquities. For as far as the heavens are above the earth, so far are His thoughts above our thoughts.

"The death of your dear brother Daniel was a dark and mysterious Providence. It almost overwhelmed me with gloom and despondency; and I thought it never could be explained to me, till I arrived at the heavenly world. But I think I can now see why it must be so. I was not sufficiently humble, nor prepared to receive the blessings which God had in store for me. Oh, that the blessed God would keep me at His feet in the very dust before Him. I never had so clear a view of the evil nature of sin, and of the glorious plan of salvation by Jesus Christ, as I have had since the death of my dear child. God has made me feel that it is an evil and bitter thing to sin against Him—that His ways are equal. And now, my dear child, I hope you will follow on to know the Lord, that you may find your going forth prepared as the morning—that His spirit may come unto you as the rain, as the latter and the former rain unto the earth.

"So prays your rejoicing, affectionate mother,

"ELIZABETH LOVEJOY."

CHAPTER IV.

Early religious editorial articles—Articles on Transubstantiation
and Nunneries..

Among the early editorial articles of Mr. Lovejoy were
two, which, being published in a city (St. Louis) where there
was a large and influential body of Roman Catholics, provoked the first opposition his paper had encountered.
They are on the doctrine of transubstantiation, and the
subject of nunneries, as follows:

"TRANSUBSTANTIATION.

"There is one plain argument against this doctrine, which
can never be set aside:

" 1. We are required to believe that the consecrated
bread and wine are really the flesh and blood of the Lord
Jesus Christ, because the Bible says, or rather the Saviour
speaks in the Bible, 'This' (that is, the bread,) 'is my
body,' and 'This' (that is, the wine,) 'is my blood.' Now,
supposing I ask, how am I to know the Bible says any
such thing? The priest opens the book and shows me the
very words, 'This is my body.' But now I ask to *see* the
bread and the wine thus metamorphosed. The priest
gives me the wafer, I taste it, it *tastes* like bread; I smell
it, it *smells* like bread; I handle it, it feels like bread.
And so of the wine.

" 2. I therefore turn to the priest and say, here are three
senses to one in favor of these elements being bread and

wine still; I am, therefore, bound to believe them so. I *can not*, from the very laws of my being, believe one sense in preference to three. I am, therefore, bound to seek some other fair interpretation of the words, 'This is my body,' than the one you have given them, or else reject them altogether. And here I need be at no loss. Turning to John, x. 9, I find Jesus saying, 'I am the door;' and in John, xv. 1, he says, 'I am the true vine,' yet you do not pretend to make the Saviour literally say that he was a door or a vine. Or if he had, when speaking to his disciples, intended to be understood literally, and they had so understood his meaning, they *could* not have believed him. They heard him say so, but they smelled, saw, and felt that he was not so, and, consequently, must distrust their own hearing or his veracity. And the case would be the same when sitting with him at the supper of the passover. If he declared to them that they were eating and drinking flesh and blood, they could only know that he did so by the sense of hearing, whereas, by three senses, taste, touch, and smell, they would be assured they were doing no such thing. According to the very laws of the human mind, therefore, they could not so understand him.

"3. The only remark we have to make upon this argument is, that no man, in his senses, ever believed fully and fairly the doctrine of transubstantiation. It is impossible that he should do so. He might as well believe that fire is cold and ice is hot, or that a thing is and is not at the same time. Let us not be misunderstood; there have, doubtless, been many men who honestly *thought* they believed it, but, owing to the prejudice of education, their minds, in this point, was dark, and saw things that were not as though they were. So often do we see individuals afflicted with mental imbecility on some particular subject, but perfectly sane on every other. In this way we can account for the fact that many good men have unquestionably *supposed* they believed the doctrine of transubstatiation; a dogma which, if true, makes, as has been well said, every other truth a lie..

"NUNNERIES.

"That these institutions should ever have acquired any favor in a community so shrewd, sagacious, and suspicious as the American people are, is truly a wonder. And that they should have succeeded in obtaining inmates from the families of Protestants, and even members of the church, is still more astonishing. It is to be accounted for on no common principle of human action. In this, as in other things, Romanism has shown itself a ' mystery of iniquity.'

"What is a nunnery? Have the American people ever asked themselves this question? And if so, have they ever reflected long enough upon it to obtain an answer satisfactory to their own mind? What is a nunnery, we ask again? We will tell. It is a dwelling whose inmates consists of unmarried females of all ages, tempers, dispositions, and habits. These females have entered into *voluntary* vows of *chastity*, *poverty*, and *obedience* to the rules of their order and their spiritual superiors. They have been induced to take these vows and exclude themselves from the world, from various motives. Some whose affections were young and ardent, from disappointment of the heart;

some from love of retirement; some from morbid sensitiveness to the world of society, and some others from the blandishments of priest and lady-superiors.   In Europe, there is another cause—operating more than any other, perhaps than all others—-which people the convents.   Unfeeling parents make them the receptacle of those daughters, who may be in the way of the aggrandizement of other members of the family, or who may be disposed to contract an alliance which they will not approve.   This, too, is probably a remote cause of many entering convents in this country.

"Very well; now let us take a convent whose inmates have been brought together from causes like the above. There are the aged, the middle-aged, the young, the ardent, the beautiful.   Thus much concerning them we all know.

"But one of these communities issues, through their superior, to the community in which it is situated, proposals for taking young ladies as inmates in their dwelling and educating them there.   This is all well enough.   But now, suppose a Protestant parent, before committing his daughters to their guardianship, visits the convent to learn something of its character.   He finds it situated in a retired place, surrounded with a high wall, embosomed in luxurious groves.   All the charms of nature and art are combined to render its retreat inviting and its bowers alluring. Into one room only can the visitant have access.   Labyrinthian passages, in various directions, lead to appartments never to be profaned by a Protestant eye.

"All here is seclusion and mystery.   These doors are

locked, and neither parent, brother, friend, nor even sister, can turn the key. Yet to this rigid exclusion there is one exception. The Caltholic priest is privileged to come at all hours, and on all occasions, as may suit his convenience. He has the 'open sesame,' before which the door of every department flies open, and admits him to familiar, unrestrained intercourse with its inmates. But who is the Catholic priest? Is he aged, venerable? Is he even a married man? No; he is (or may be) a young man, and like those whom he visits, bound by his vow to a life of celibacy. And whatever his *vow* may have been, his looks show abundantly that fasting, penance, and mortifying of the body make no part of his *practice.* His is not the lean and subdued countenance of the penitent, but the jolly visage of the sensualist rather. Alas! for the ladies of the convent, if his vow of chastity is kept no better than his vow of poverty and penance. And what reason have we to suppose it is? If he violate it in one case, why not in the other? The temptation is, at least, as great.

We will present this subject in a little different light. Suppose a dozen young ministers from the Theological Seminary of Princeton, having just been ordained, should come out and take up their abode in the City of St. Louis. Suppose some one of our wealthy citizens, or, if you please, citizens of Boston, or New York, should furnish them with the funds requisite to put up a building in some retired place in the outskirts of the town; supposing the building finished, furnished, enclosed with a high wall, evidently intended for exclusion. Suppose now the young gentlemen advertise in the newspapers of the city that they have brought with them, from Boston, a dozen young ladies who have each made a solemn promise that they will never marry, and that these ladies are now in the newly-erected building, prepared to open a school, and to receive female pupils as boarders. Suppose they also should make it known that these young ladies had chosen one of their own number*—or perhaps the arrangement might be that they should take turns in performing this office, but always so that but one at a time should be at the house—to be their father confessor, and that he was to have access to their dwelling at any or all times, coming and going unquestioned, and that he, or certainly his fellows, were to be the only males who should have access to, or authority in, the establishment. All this being perfectly understood, let us, for the last time, suppose that one of these young gentlemen should go round to the respectable families of our city and solicit that their daughters might become the inmates, as pupils, of their establishment. What reception would he be likely to meet with? How many young ladies would he be likely to collect for his school? Yet, gentle reader, suppose all the above conditions fulfilled, and you have a Protestant convent or nunnery, formed, in all its essential features, on the most-approved model of the Romanists. Who would trust a dozen Protestant ministers, under such circumstances as these? No one. And, indeed, the very fact that they asked to be trusted would prove them all unworthy. But do the annals of the church show that the Popish priesthood are more worthy of trust, purer, holier than the Protestant clergy? Read "Scipio de

* One of the young men.

Ricci," and "Blanco White;" read "Secreta Monita" of
the Jesuits, "Bower's History of the Popes," and "Text
Book of Popery," or if these will not convince, read Hume,
Gibbon, Robertson, or even Lingard himself—read Ros-
coe's Leo the Tenth; nay, their own approved manuals of
faith and practice. Read these and know that corruption,
rank and foul, has always steamed, and is now steaming
from the thousand monasteries, convents, and nunneries
that are spread, like so many plague-spots, over the surface
of Europe.

We do not say, for we do not believe, that they have
reached the same degree of pollution in this country. Far
from it; and yet we are no advocates of, or believers in,
their immaculate purity. But what we say is this, that so
long as human nature remains as it is, so long will the *tendency*, the unavoidable tendency, of such institutions be to
iniquity and corruption. We care not in whose hands they
are, Popish or Protestant, they tempt to sin all who are
connected with them. We might even admit that they
were founded with good intentions—which, in many instances, we have no doubt has been the case—and still
our objections to them would be no whit lessened. Talk
of vows of chastity in chambers of impenetrable seclusion, and amidst bowers of voluptuousness and beauty!
'Tis a shameful mockery, and especially with the record
of history spread out before us. For that informs us that
the nunnery has generally been neither more nor less than
a seraglio for the friars of the monastery.

CHAPTER V.

His views on Colonization and Gradual Emancipation, as he first held them.

In common with many good citizens of Missouri, Mr. Lovejoy looked forward to the State Convention, appointed for Dec., 1835, in hope that some action would then be taken to secure gradual emancipation. He felt it to be right, as the editor of a religious paper, to open his columns for the temperate discussion of the subject, and to present his own views in the editorial columns. From one of his articles, dated 16th April, 1835, it will be seen that *The St. Louis Republican*, the leading commercial paper of the State, held similar views, at that time, to those of Mr. Lovejoy upon the subject:

SLAVERY.

We ask from every professor of Christianity, as also from all others, a careful, candid, and *prayerful* perusal of the article on our first page on this subject. It is from the pen of one* who is entitled to be heard in the case; inasmuch as having been a slave-holder once, he has ceased to be such by emancipating all his slaves.

The main principles, facts, and inferences stated by the writer, we are so far from questioning, that we believe them entirely correct.

"How hardly shall they that have riches be saved," said

* The article is signed "N.," presumed to be from Dr. Nelson, author of "Nelson on Infidelity."

One who perfectly well knew the principles by which the
human mind operated and was operated upon. For the
same reason, though found in the opposite extreme, we
may say how hardly shall they that are slaves enter into
the kingdom of heaven. In either case there is nothing
which absolutely forbids heaven to either class, or which
renders it of itself more difficult of attainment, yet, judg-
ing from analogy and from the results of experience, we
are enabled confidently to predict that not "many wise,
not many noble," and not many ignorant slaves will make
their way through the difficulties that surround their posi-
tions, to a heaven of disinterestedness and intelligence.

While therefore we cordially adopt the main sentiments
of our correspondent, and would affectionately, yet urgent-
ly, press them upon our Christian readers as a reason why
they should introduce a thorough change in their manner
of treating, or rather neglecting, their slaves, so far as
religious instruction is concerned; we do not believe that
this change ought to be *immediate and unconditional emancipation.* We are entirely convinced that such a course
would be cruel to the slave himself, and injurious to the
community at large. But something must be done and
done speedily on this all-important subject. While Christians have been slumbering over it, the eye of God has not
slumbered, nor has his justice been an indifferent spectator
of the scene. The groans, and sighs, and tears, and blood
of the poor slave have gone up as a memorial before the
throne of heaven. In due time they will descend in awful
curses upon this land, unless averted by the speedy repentance of us all

Look at the manner in which our sister State, Louisiana, is treating her slaves! Why, as surely as there is a thunder-bolt in heaven and strength in God's right arm to launch it, so surely will it strike the authors of such cruel oppression. Look, too, at the *slave-drivers*, who go up and down our own streets, lifting their heads and moving among us unshamed, unrebuked,—as if they had not forfeited all claim to the name of *man*. All abhor the traffic, and detest the wretch who pursues it; why then is he not driven from the face of day, and made to hide himself in some dark corner, whose mirky gloom might faintly emblem the savage darkness of his own heart? Why? simply because public sentiment has never been aroused to think on the subject. If the laws protect the miscreant who coins his wealth out of the heart's blood of his fellow-creatures, he can at least be crushed beneath the odium of public opinion.

There is another fact we wish to introduce in this place. It is this: Congress, acting only as the organ of public opinion, has pronounced the slave-trade from the coast of Africa *piracy*. Those engaged in it are punishable with death. From a statement given in the *Journal of Commerce*, it appears that last November, there were no less than *forty-eight* slave vessels on the African coast engaged in this nefarious traffic. It was supposed these vessels would carry off at least 20,000 victims,—victims in every sense of the term, to tyranny, brutality, and lust.

It also appears that many of these poor wretches eventually land in the United States by way of Cuba and other Spanish islands. Particularly is it to be feared and supposed that many of them are smuggled into Louisiana. Now, although the system of domestic slavery is not necessarily connected with this foreign piratical trade, yet no one can deny that it tends greatly to encourage it. And no one can deny, that if domestic slavery should cease throughout Christendom, the slave-trade from Africa would cease of course. We mention these things as affording strong incidental reasons for action among ourselves at home. Above all the rest, the same paper states that there is no doubt a slave-vessel left New York a few days since.

In this connection it gives us heartfelt pleasure to introduce the following extract from *The Republican* of Friday last. The editors are referring to the convention about to be called for the purpose of amending our constitution. With the sentiments of the extract we most cordially concur, and hope the editors will not fail to keep the subject before their readers till the time for action shall arrive. And who are the individuals, or individual, who will make it their business between the present time and the time for voting, to arouse and enlighten public sentiment on this great subject? What a glorious opportunity is now offered to such a one—an opportunity such as will not be likely again to arise for centuries to come—to confer a lasting, an unspeakable benefit upon the citizens of this State, of this republic, and upon the cause of universal humanity! Is it too much to ask of Christians, that they will ask the Lord, in fervent, importunate prayer, to send such a laborer into the field of this State? We do not want a man from the northern or middle States; we want one who has himself been educated in the midst of slavery, who has always lived in contact with it, who knows, experimentally, all its evils, and all its difficulties,—one who will not lift his head up into the region of abstract speculation, and in the loftiness of his pride, in a beautiful theory, disdain alike to make acquaintance with facts and with common-sense. To such a man a golden opportunity of doing good is offered. We believe the minds of the good people of this State are fully prepared to listen to him,—to give a dispassionate consideration to the facts and reasonings he might present connected with the subject of slavery.

Public sentiment, amongst us, is already moving in this great matter—it now wants to be directed in some defined channel, to some definite end.

Taking all in all, there is not a State in this Union possessing superior natural advantages to our own. At present, slavery, like an incubus, is paralyzing our energies, and like a cloud of evil portent, darkening all our prospects. Let this be removed, and Missouri would at once start forward in the race of improvement, with an energy and rapidity of movement that would soon place her in the front rank along with the most favored of her sister States. But we stay too long from the extract from *The Republican:*

"We look to the convention as a happy means of relieving the State, at some future day, of an evil which is destroying all our wholesome energies, and leaving us, in morals, in enterprise, and in wealth, behind the neighboring States. We mean, of course, the curse of *slavery*. We are not about to make any attack upon the rights of those who at present hold this description of property. They ought to be respected to the letter. We only propose that measures shall now be taken for the *abolition of slavery*, at such distant period of time as may be thought expedient, and eventually for ridding the country altogether of a colored population. The plan has been adopted in other States, and they have been effectually relieved from the incubus which, even now, is weighing us down. With no decided advantage in soil, climate, productions, or facilities, the free States have shot far ahead of those in which slavery is tolerated. We need go no further than Ohio and Kentucky for an illustration of this assertion. For ourselves, if this one principle shall be adopted, whatever may be the errors of the convention— no matter with how many absurdities the Constitution may abound, we shall gladly overlook them all. To secure so important a benefit, we must set about it at once. Now is the time for action. The evil of which we are speaking may be arrested in its incipient stage. It is, perhaps, the last time we shall have an opportunity of attempting it. And we call upon all citizens, of whatever rank, sect, or party, to aid in this good and glorious work. It is one in which all, laying aside minor controversies and considerations, may unite, and all may exert a favorable influence. Let us to the work then firmly and heartily!"

Mr. Lovejoy continued to publish editorials in favor of gradual emancipation, expressing his views firmly, but with great modesty, as will be seen in the following, dated 30th April, 1835:

" SLAVERY.

" There can be no doubt that this subject, in its various bearings, will occupy much of the attention of the good people of this State, the ensuing season. We take it for granted there will be a convention of the people at the time designated by our Legislature, (next December,) for the purpose of amending our Constitution. This convention will afford an opportunity for again deciding the question whether Missouri shall hereafter be a free or continue a slave state. We look upon this question as one of more importance than we have words to express. And in its discussion and final decision by the convention, we feel how much need there is of mutual forbearance among all those who shall have a word to say on the subject, as well as the exercise of that calm, sagacious, patriotic foresight which looks to the good of the whole community, and consults for the good of future as of present generations.

Let an unbiased, intelligent decision of our fellow-citizens in the matter be had, and we have no fears of the result. We know very well that a right decision of the case will, in many instances, have to be made in the face of immediate personal interest; but we look with confidence to the intelligence, the good sense, and the moral justice of our citizens as fully adequate to the crisis.

" Slavery, as it exists among us, admits of being considered in a three-fold view—in a civil, a religious, and a moral view. Considered in any of these lights, it is demonstrably an evil. In every community where it exists, it presses like a nightmare on the body politic. Or, like the vampire, it slowly and imperceptibly sucks away the life-blood of society, leaving it faint and disheartened to stagger along the road of improvement. Look at Virginia—that noble commonwealth, the mother of States and great men—how strikingly does her present condition illustrate the truth of this sentiment.

"The evils of slavery, in a moral and religious point of view, need not be told; they are seen, and palpably, by all.

"It becomes us, as a Christian people, as those who believe in the future retribution of a righteous Providence, to remove from our midst an institution, no less the cause of moral corruption to the master than to the slave. It surely can not be thought wrong to press such a notion as this upon the consideration of our fellow-citizens.

"Gradual emancipation is the remedy we propose. This we look upon as the only feasible, and indeed, the only desirable way of effecting our release from the thraldom in which we are held. In the meantime, the rights of all classes of our citizens should be respected, and the work be proposed, carried on, and finished, as one in which all classes of our citizens are alike interested, and in which all may alike be called upon to make sacrifices of individual interests to the general welfare of the community.

"There is, however, another matter—and we mention it here, lest our silence may be misinterpreted—connected with this subject, which admits, nay, demands a very different mode of treatment. We mean the manner in which the relations subsisting between Christians and their slaves are fulfilled. Here the reform ought to be thorough and immediate. There is no possible plea which can afford excuse for a moment's delay.

"On this point we expect to have much to say, and we hope our readers will bear in mind—and thus save themselves from confounding our arguments on the two points— that while on the general subject of slavery we are decidedly gradual, on this part of it we are as decidedly immediate abolitionists. It is fearfully true that many professed Christians habitually treat their slaves as though they had no immortal souls, and it is high time such a practice as this were *abolished.*"

CHAPTER VI.

Excitement at St. Louis—An article on Slavery—Lovejoy's sympathy with the masters—Public feeling rising—White men
whipped—Prominent citizens counsel Mr. Lovejoy to cease
discussing the subject of Slavery

During the summer of 1835, Mr. Lovejoy continued to
publish articles in the *St. Louis Observer*, on the subject of
slavery. He exhibited no little sympathy for the masters,
as well as the slaves, and disapproved heated and angry
discussion of the subject, as appears by the following from
his paper in the month of June. He was then in favor of
colonization and gradual emancipation :

"SLAVERY.

"This subject is one which has always, since we have
known anything of the Southern and Slave-holding Western States, been regarded as exceedingly delicate and difficult of management. We feel it to be so at the moment of
penning these remarks. Not because—as some of our
Abolitionist brethren will charge us—we fear the truth,
and are unwilling to perform our duty, but, because there
is real difficulty in ascertaining what that duty is. The
man who has been reared in the midst of Slavery, and
acquainted with the system from his earliest infancy, who
regards the colored man as part of the estate bequeathed
to him by his parents, and his right over him guaranteed
by the Constitution of his country, becomes excited, when
any one denies this right, and lays down ethical principles

49

for his government, that, in their operation, must beggar
him.

"Nor is this all; he finds himself the subject of bitter in-
vective and unmeasured denunciation. As a man, stripped
of all honorable pretension, and made a participant with
the heartless man-stealer, whose crime he abhors. As a
Christian, denounced and accounted a profaner of the sym-
bols of his holy religion. Held up to society as a monster
in human shape, a tyrant who delights in the pangs inflicted upon his fellow-man. We have never wondered that
under such circumstances, it should be an exciting subject—
he must be more than human who would not be sensible
of the recoil in his feelings.

"He may at the same time be wrong. But his early associations—his prejudices, are all upon the side of long-estab-
lished opinions; and hence it should hardly be expected,
that, at the first glance, he should see the truth as one
differently situated, may see it, and instantly espousing the
opinion of the opposite party, give an evidence of his sincerity that the other was never called to give, by passing
immediately from affluence to poverty. In all controversies, there is a strong tendency in the parties to take extreme ground—so in this—and hence he finds himself
charged with views and feelings, and base motives for his
opposition, which he is at the moment conscious he does
not possess, and which the very man who presses the
charge against him, in his cooler moments, would not think
of making. Certain it is, that in this controversy, no one
will be persuaded by naked denunciation or misrepresentations—but cool and temperate argument, supported by
facts, must perform the work.

"It has been with pain that we have seen, recently, the heated and angry meetings and discussions which have taken place amongst our eastern brethren of the Abolition and Colonization parties."

INCREASE OF EXCITEMENT.

The abolition excitement increased every day during the summer of 1835. Slave-holders, at St. Louis, became unwilling to permit any one to address, "cool and temperate arguments" to them on the subject of Slavery. Mr. Lovejoy's articles, therefore, though conceived in a Christian spirit, were very offensive. Not a word must be said— the silence of death would alone satisfy them, while he demanded free speech. The difference was irreconcilable. Obloquy and reproach were heaped upon him. The rabble called him—with a curse—an amalgamationist, and threatened to destroy his office: slave-holders were ready to tar and feather him as an Abolitionist, and no man ventured to defend him in that city. In this state of things, Mr. Lovejoy's clerical duties led him to leave St. Louis for about three weeks, to attend Synod and Presbytery.

The excitement was so great that the prudent proprietors of the *St. Louis Observer*, and its St. Louis patrons, published a card, advising the publishers to entirely suspend "all controversy on the exciting subject of slavery." The publishers assented to this until Mr. Lovejoy should return, when the question was to be laid before him. At this time the excitement was further increased by the action of gentlemen, who were pronounced by the proprietors of the *Observer*, as "several of the most respectable citizens of St. Louis." These "respectable citizens" had caught two white men, who were suspected of having decoyed away slaves, and had taken them two miles back of the city to be either whipped or hung for this offence. Only twenty out of sixty of these "respectable citizens" voted for hanging, and consequently the more merciful punishment, was bestowed of from one hundred to two hundred lashes each. These "wealthy and influential citizens," some of whom were church-members, took turns in the whipping, and this action was thenceforth called proceeding "under the new code." Does the reader ask whether such things were allowed by the civil authority? They were gloried in by those who held the power and winked at by civil authority.

The proprietors of the *Observer*, Lovejoy being still absent, were frightened, and again publicly announced that nothing should be advanced in the paper calculated to keep up the excitement on the slavery question.

They stated that they had heard with astonishment and regret the rumors of the intended destruction of the *Observer* office, and they "called on all prudent men to pause and reflect on the consequences of such a step." The following letter was addressed to Mr. Lovejoy by some of the worthiest gentlemen in the city, including the excellent Pastor and two of the Elders of the Second Presbyterian Church:

PROMINENT CITIZENS PUBLICLY COUNSEL LOVEJOY.

"ST. LOUIS, October 5th, 1835.

"*To the Rev. E. P. Lovejoy, Editor of the Observer.*

"SIR: The undersigned, friends and supporters of the *Observer*, beg leave to suggest, that the present temper of the times requires a change in the manner of conducting that print in relation to the subject of domestic slavery.

"The public mind is greatly excited, and owing to the unjustifiable interference of our northern brethren with our social relations, the community are, perhaps, not in a situation to endure sound doctrine in relation to this subject. Indeed, we have reason to believe that violence is even now meditated against the *Observer* office and we do believe that true policy and the interests of religion require that the discussion of this exciting question should be at least postponed in this State.

"Although we do not claim the right to prescribe your course as an editor, we hope that the concurring opinions of so many persons, having the interests of your paper and of religion, both at heart, may induce you to distrust your own judgment, and so far change the character of the *Observer*, as to pass over in silence everything connected with the subject of slavery; we would like that you announce in your paper your intention so to do.

"We shall be glad to be informed of your determination in relation to this matter.

"Respectfully, your obedient servants,

ARCHIBALD GAMBLE,
NATHAN RANNEY,
WILLIAM S. POTTS,
JOHN KERR,
G. W. CALL,
H. R. GAMBLE,
HEZEKIAH KING.

"I concur in the object intended by this communication.

"BEVERLY ALLEN."

"I concur in the foregoing.

"J. B. BRANT."

More than two years after the date of this letter, and precisely two weeks before his death, Lovejoy endorsed upon it the following solemn declaration:

"I did not yield to the wishes here expressed, and in consequence have been persecuted ever since. But I have kept a good conscience in the matter, and that repays me for all I have suffered, or can suffer. I have sworn eternal opposition to slavery, and by the blessing of God, I will never go back."

"E. P. L. October 24, 1837."

CHAPTER VII.

Public meeting to oppose the discussion—Lovejoy's defence of
his course.

About this time, Oct., 1835, Mr. Lovejoy was falsely
charged with the mortal offence of transmitting abolition
newspapers to Jefferson City, boxed and ready for distri-
bution in Missouri. Agitation, consequently, increased,
and there was a public meeting on the subject of the course
pursued by the opposers of slavery, at which the following
Resolutions, among others, were passed:

"2. *Resolved*, That the right of free discussion and freedom of speech exists under the Constitution, but that being a conventional reservation made by the people in their
sovereign capacity, does not imply a moral right on the
part of the Abolitionists to freely discuss the question of
Slavery, either orally or through the medium of the press.
It is the agitation of a question too nearly allied to the vital
interests of the slave-holding States to admit of public dis-
putation; and so far from the fact, that the movements of
the Abolitionists are constitutional, they are in the greatest
degree seditious, and calculated to incite insurrection and
anarchy, and ultimately, a disseverment of our prosperous
Union.

"3. *Resolved*, That we consider the course pursued by the
Abolitionists, as one calculated to paralyze every social tie
by which we are now united to our fellow-man, and that,
if persisted in, it must eventually be the cause of the dis-

severment of these United States; and that the doctrine of
amalgamation is peculiarly baneful to the interests and
happiness of society.   The union of black and white, in a
moral point of view, we consider as the most preposterous
and impudent doctrine advanced by the infatuated Abolitionist, as repugnant to judgment and science, as it is
degrading to the feelings of all sensitive minds—as destructive to the intellect of after generations, as the advance
of science and literature has contributed to the improvement of our own.   In short, its practice would reduce the
high intellectual standard of the American mind to a level
with the Hottentot, and the United States, now second to
no nation on earth, would, in a few years, be what Europe
was in the darkest ages.

"4. *Resolved*, That the sacred writings furnish abundant
evidence of the existence of slavery from the earliest
periods.   The patriarchs and prophets possessed slaves—
our Saviour recognized the relation between master and
slave, and deprecated it not: hence, we know that He did
not condemn that relation; on the contrary, His disciples,
in all countries, designated their respective duties to each
other; Therefore,

"*Resolved*, That we consider slavery, as it now exists in
the United States, as sanctioned by the Sacred Scriptures."

LOVEJOY'S PUBLIC DEFENCE AND REPLY TO THE
CITIZENS' RESOLUTIONS.

After the receipt of the letter from Mr. Gamble and
others, and after the passage in a public meeting of the
resolutions just recited, Mr. Lovejoy felt impelled to make
a public appeal to his fellow-citizens in reply, the principal
portions of which are as follows:

"NOVEMBER 5TH, 1835.

"To my Fellow-Citizens:

"Recent well-known occurrences in this city, and else-where, have, in the opinion of some of my friends, as well as my own, made it my duty to address myself to you personally. And, in so doing, I hope to be pardoned for that apparent egotism which, in such an address, is more or less unavoidable. I hope, also, to write in that spirit of meekness and humility that becomes a follower of the Lamb; and, at the same time, with all that boldness and sincerity of speech which should mark the language of a freemàn and a Christian minister. It is not my design or wish to offend any one, but simply to maintain my rights as a republican citizen, free-born, of these United States, and to defend, fearlessly, the cause of truth and righteousness."

(Here follows an explanation of his sentiments on the subject of slavery, already sufficiently indicated.)

"And now, fellow-citizens, having made the above explation, for the purpose of undeceiving such of you as have honestly supposed me in error; truth and candor require me to add, that had I desired to send a copy of the *Emancipator*, or of any other newspaper, to Jefferson City, I should not have taken the pains to box it up. I am not aware that any law of my country forbids my sending what document I please to a friend or citizen. I know, indeed, that *mob law* has decided otherwise, and that it has become fashionable, in certain parts of this country, to break open the post-office, and take from it such documents as the mob should decide, ought not to pass *unburned*. But I had never imagined there was a sufficiency of respectability attached to the proceeding, to recommend it for adoption to the good citizens of my own State. And grievously and sadly shall I be disappointed to find it otherwise.

"In fine, I wish it to be distinctly understood, that I have never, knowingly, to the best of my recollection, sent a single copy of the *Emancipator*, or any other Abolition publication, to a single individual in Missouri, or elsewhere; while yet I claim the *right* to send ten thousand of them if I choose, to as many of my fellow-citizens. Whether I will *exercise* that right or not, is for me, and not for the *mob*, to decide. The right to send publications of any sort to slaves, or in any way to communicate with them, without the *express permission* of their masters, I freely acknowledge that I have not. Nor do I wish to have it. It is with the master alone, that I would have to do, as one freeman with another; and who shall say me nay?

"I come now to the proceedings had at the late meetings of our citizens. And in discussing them, I hope not to say a single word that shall wound the feelings of a single individual concerned. It is with principles I have to do, and not with men. And in canvassing them, freely, openly, I do but exercise a right secured by the solemn sanction of the Constitution, to the humblest citizen of this republic —a right that, so long as life lasts, I do not expect to relinquish.

"I freely acknowledge the respectability of the citizens who composed the meetings referred to. And were the questions under consideration, to be decided as mere matters of opinion, it would become me, however much I might differ from them, to bow in humble silence to the decisions of such a body of my fellow-citizens. But I can not surrender my principles, though the whole world besides should vote them down—I can make no compromise between truth and error, even though my life be the alternative.

"Of the first resolution passed at the meeting of the 24th of October, I have nothing to say, except that I perfectly agree with the sentiment, that the citizens of the non-slaveholding States have no right to interfere with the domestic relations between master and slave.

"The second resolution, strictly speaking, neither affirms nor denies anything in reference to the matter in hand. No man has a *moral* right to do any thing improper. Whether, therefore, he has the moral right to discuss the question of slavery, is a point with which human legislation or resolutions have nothing to do. The true issue to be decided is, whether he has the *civil*, the political right, to discuss it or not. And this is a mere question of fact. In Russia, in Turkey, in Austria, nay, even in France, this right most certainly does not exist. But does it exist in Missouri? We decide this question by turning to the Constitution of the State. The Sixteenth Section, Article Thirteenth, of the Constitution of Missouri, reads as follows:

"'That the free communication of thoughts and opinions is one of the invaluable rights of man, and that every person may freely speak, write, and print *on any subject*, being responsible for the abuse of that liberty.'

"Here, then, I find my warrant for using, as Paul did, all freedom of speech.

"If I abuse that right, I freely acknowledge myself amenable to the laws.

"But it is said, that the right to hold slaves is a constitutional one, and, therefore, not be called in question. I admit the premise, but deny the conclusion. To put a strong case by way of illustration. The Constitution declares that this shall be a perpetual Republic; but has not any citizen the right to discuss, under that Constitution, the comparative merits of despotism and liberty? And if he has eloquence and force of argument sufficient, may he not persuade us all to crown him our king? Robert Dale Owen came to this city, and Fanny Wright followed him, openly proclaiming the doctrine that the institution of marriage was a curse to any community, and ought to be abolished. It was, undoubtedly, an abominable doctrine, and one which, if acted out, would speedily reduce society to the level of barbarism and the brutes; yet, who thought of denying Mr. Owen and his disciple the perfect right of avowing such doctrines, or who thought of mobbing them for the exercise of this right? And yet, most surely, the institutions of slavery are not more interwoven with the structure of our society, than those of marriage.

"See the danger, and the natural and inevitable result, to which the first step here will lead. To-day, a public meeting declares that you shall not discuss the subject of slavery in any of its bearings, civil or religious. Right or wrong, the press must be silent. To-morrow, another meeting decides that it is against the peace of society, that the principles of Popery shall be discussed, and the edict goes forth to muzzle the press. The next day, it is, in a similar manner, declared that not a word must be said against distilleries, dram-shops, or drunkenness. And so on to the end of the chapter. The truth is, my fellow-citizens, if you give ground a single inch, there is no stopping place. I deem it, therefore, my duty to take my stand upon the Constitution. Here is firm ground—I feel it to be such. And I do most respectfully, yet decidedly, declare to you my fixed determination to maintain this ground. We have slaves, it is true, but *I* am not one. I am a citizen of these United States, a citizen of Missouri, free-born; and having never forfeited the inestimable privileges attached to such a condition, I can not consent to surrender them. But while I maintain them, I hope to do it with all that meekness and humility that become a Christian, and especially a Christian minister. I am ready, not to fight, but to suffer, and if need be, to die for them. Kindred blood to that which flows in my veins, flowed freely to water the tree of Christian liberty, planted by the Puritans on the rugged soil of New England. It flowed as freely on the plains of Lexington, the heights of Bunker Hill, and fields of Saratoga. And freely, too, shall mine flow, yea, as freely as if it were so much water, ere I surrender my right to plead the cause of truth and righteousness before my fellow-citizens, and in the face of all their opposers.

"Of the third resolution I must be allowed to say, that I have never seen the least evidence, whatever, that the Abolitionists, with all their errors, have ever desired to effect an amalgamation of the two races,—black and white. I respectfully ask of the individuals composing the meeting that adopted this resolution, if they have ever seen any such evidence?

"They have formally, solemnly, and officially denied it. It is certainly an abhorrent thing even in theory, and a thousand times more so in practice. And yet, unless my eyes deceive me, as I walk the streets of our city, there are some among us who venture to put it into practice. And, in the appointment of the numerous committees of vigilance, superintendence, etc., methinks that not one of them all was more needed than a committee whose business it should be to ferret out, from their secret 'chambers of iniquity,' these practical amalgamationists. If He who said to the woman taken in adultery, 'Go and sin no more,' had stood in the midst of the meeting at our Court-House, I will not say that he would there have detected a single amalgamator; but I am sure that if a poor Abolitionist were to be stoned in St. Louis for holding this preposterous notion, and the same rule were to be applied that our Saviour used in the case referred to, there are at least some amongst us who could not cast a pebble at the sinner's head.

"What shall I, what can I, say of the fourth resolution? It was adopted, in a large assemblage of my fellow-citizens, with but a few dissenting voices. Many of our most respectable citizens voted for it—Presbyterians, Methodists, Baptists, Episcopalians, Roman Catholics; those who believe the bible is the word of God and those who do not, all united in voting for the resolution that the bible sanctions slavery as it now exists in the United States. If the sentiment had been that the bible sanctions the con-

tinuance of the system until proper measures can be taken
to remove it, I too could adopt it.

"If I have taken my neighbor's property and spent it,
and afterwards repent of my sin, and wish to restore what
I had unjustly taken, but have not the means, the bible
no longer holds me as a thief, but sanctions my withhold-
ing the money from my neighbor, until I can, by the use
of the best means in my power, obtain it and restore it.
And although, meanwhile, my neighbor, in consequence of
my original crime, may be deprived of his rights, and his
family made to suffer all the evils of poverty and shame,
the bible would still enjoin it upon him to let me alone,
nay, to forgive me, and even to be content in the abject
condition to which I had reduced him. Even so the bible
now says to our slaves, as it said in the days of the apostles, 'Servants (or slaves), obey in all things your masters
according to the flesh; not with eye-service, as men-
pleasers, but in singleness of heart, fearing God.' But then
it also adds, 'Masters, give unto your servants that which
is just and equal.' What is meant by 'just and equal' we
may learn from the Saviour himself: 'All things whatso-
ever ye would that men should do unto you, do ye even so
to them ; for this is the law and the prophets.' Thus far
the bible. And it will be seen, that in no case does it
sanction, but the rather, absolutely forbids, all insurrec-
tionary, all seditious, all rebellious acts on the part of the
slaves. But, be it remembered, that, with equal decision
and authority, it says to the master, 'Undo the heavy
burden, and let the oppressed go free.' If either disobey
these injunctions, then it bids us leave the whole matter

with that God who declares: 'Vengeance is mine, I will repay, saith the Lord.'

"But I am not at liberty so to understand the resolution. From the preamble, and from conversation with several who voted for it, I am compelled to understand the meeting as voting that the bible—the blessed Saviour and his holy apostles—sanctions the principle of slavery—the system itself, as such, as it now exists amongst us.

"Fellow-citizens! I mean not to be disrespectful to you, but I declare before you all, I have not words to express my utter abhorrence of such a sentiment. My soul detests it, my heart sickens over it; my judgment, my understanding, my conscience, reject it, with loathing and horror.

"What is the system of slavery 'as it now exists in the United States?' It is a system of buying and selling immortal beings for the sake of gain; a system which forbids to man and woman the rights of husband and wife, sanctioning the dissolution of this tie at the mere caprice of another; a system which tolerates the existence of a class of men whose professed business it is to go about from house to house, tearing husband and wife, parent and child asunder, chaining their victims together, and then driving them with a whip, like so many mules, to a distant market, there to be disposed of to the highest bidder. And then the nameless pollutions, the unspeakable abominations, that attend this unfortunate class in their cabins. But I spare the details. And this is the system sanctioned by the Prince of Mercy and Love, by the God of Holiness and Purity! Oh, God! In the language of one of the patriarchs to whom the meeting in their resolution refer,

I say, 'Oh, my soul, come not thou into their secret, unto their assembly mine honour be not thou united!'

"The fifth resolution appoints a committee of vigilance, consisting of seven for each ward, twenty for the suburbs, and seven for each township in the county,—in all, eighty-three persons,—whose duty it shall be to report to the mayor, or the other civil authorities, all persons *suspected* of preaching Abolition doctrines, etc., and should the civil authorities fail to deal with them, on *suspicion*, why, then, the committee are to call a meeting of the citizens and execute their decrees—in other words, to *lynch* the suspected persons.

"Fellow-citizens; where are we, and in what age of the world do we live? Is this the land of freedom or despotism? Is it the ninth or nineteenth century? Have the principles of the *lettres de cachet*, driven from Europe, crossed the Atlantic and taken up their abode in Missouri? Louis the XIV. sent men to the Bastile on suspicion; we, more humane, do but whip them to death, or nearly so. But these things can not last long. A few may be made the innocent victims of lawless violence, yet, be assured, there is a moral sense in the Christendom of the nineteenth century, that will not long endure such odious transactions. A tremendous reaction will take place.

"And remember, I pray you, that as Phalaris was the first man roasted in the brazen bull he had constructed for the tyrant of Sicily, so the inventor of the guillotine was by no means the last whose neck had practical experience of the keenness of its edge. I turn, for a moment, to my fellow-Christians of all Protestant denominations.

"*Respected and beloved Fathers and Brethren:* As I address myself to you, my heart is full, well-nigh to bursting, and my eyes overflow. It is indeed a time of trial and rebuke. The enemies of the cross are numerous and bold and malignant in the extreme. From the situation in which the providence of God has placed me, a large portion of their hatred, in this quarter, has concentrated itself on me. You know that now for nearly two years, a constant stream of calumnies and personal abuse of the most viperous kind has been poured upon me, simply because I have been your organ through which—I refer now more especially to my Presbyterian brethren — you have declared your sentiments. You know, also, that I have never, in a single instance, replied to or otherwise noticed these attacks. And now, not only is a fresh attack of ten-fold virulence, made upon my character, but violence is threatened to my person. Think not that it is because I am an Abolitionist that I am so persecuted. They who first started this report knew, and still know, better. In the progress of events, slavery has, doubtless, contributed its share, though a very small one, to the bitterness of hatred with which the *Observer*, and I, as connected with it, are regarded. But the true cause is the open and decided stand which the paper has taken against the encroachments of Popery. This is not only my own opinion, but that of others, and indeed of nearly or quite all with whom I have conversed on the subject, and among the rest, as I learn, of a French Catholic. I repeat it, then, the real origin of the cry, ' Down with the *Observer*,' is to be looked for in its opposition to Popery. The fire that is now blazing and crackling through this city, was kindled on Popish altars, and has been assiduously blown up by Jesuit breath. And now, dear brethren, the question is, shall we flee before it, or stay and abide its fury, even though we perish in the flames? For one, I can not hesitate. The path of duty lies plain before me, and I must walk therein, even though it lead to the whipping-post, the tar-barrel, or even the stake. I was bold and dauntless in the service of sin; it is not fitting that I should be less so in the service of my Redeemer. He sought me out when there was none to help; when I was fast sinking to eternal ruin, he raised me up and placed me on the Rock of Ages; and now, shall I forsake him when he has so few friends and so many enemies in St. Louis? I can not, I dare not, and, his grace sustaining me, *I will not.*

*   *   *   *   *   *

"A few words more, and I have done. Fellow-citizens of St. Louis, above, you have my sentiments, fully and freely expressed, on the great subjects now agitating the public mind. Are they such as render me unworthy of that protection which regulated society accords to the humblest of its members? Let me ask you why is it that this storm of persecution is directed against me? What have I done? Have I libelled any man's person or character? No. Have I been found in gambling-houses, billiard-rooms, or tippling-shops? Never. Have I ever disturbed the peace and quiet of your city by midnight revellings or riots in the streets? It is not pretended. Have I ever, by word or deed, directly or indirectly, attempted or designed to incite your slaves to insubordination? God forbid. I would as soon be guilty of arson and murder.   *   *   *

"I *do*, therefore, as an American citizen, and Christian patriot, and in the name of liberty, and law, and religion, solemnly protest against all these attempts, howsoever or by whomsoever made, to frown down the liberty of the press, and forbid the free expression of public opinion. Under a deep sense of my obligations to my country, the church, and my God, I declare it to be my fixed purpose to submit to no such dictation. And I am prepared to abide the consequences. I have appealed to the constitution and laws of my country; if they fail to protect me, I appeal to God, and with Him I cheerfully rest my cause.

"Fellow-citizens, they told me that if I returned to the city, from my late absence, you would surely lay violent hands upon me, and many of my friends besought me not to come. I disregarded their advice, because I plainly saw, or thought I saw, that the Lord would have me come. And up to this moment that conviction of duty has continued to strengthen, until now I have not the shadow of a doubt that I did right. I have appeared openly among you, in your streets and market-places, and now I openly and publicly throw myself into your hands. I can die at my post, but I can not desert it.   *   *   *   *

"Humbly entreating all whom I have injured, whether intentionally or otherwise, to forgive me; in charity with all men; freely forgiving my enemies, even those who thirst for my blood, and with the blest assurance, that in life or death, nothing can separate me from my Redeemer, I subscribe myself,

"Your fellow-citizen,

"ELIJA P. LOVEJOY."

CHAPTER VIII.

The Martyr-Spirit as displayed by Mr. Lovejoy—Letter from Mr. G. T. M. Davis.

If we would appreciate correctly the sublime act of Lovejoy in issuing the foregoing appeal, from his press, we must consider the extreme danger in which he was of losing his life thereby. He wrote to his brother that, on his way from synod, reports came that the citizens were whipping men almost to death, and that no one suspected of Abolitionism could live in St. Louis. The *Observer* had been muzzled by its original proprietors. He had been accused by name, in one of the city papers, of being an Abolitionist, and public vengence had been invoked upon him in the bitterest manner. A mob had been raised to tear down the *Observer* office, but had concluded, after assembling, to defer it a little longer. Men's hearts were failing them for fear, and friends had assured him that he could not walk the streets with safety, by night or by day. His young and sick wife was the only friend that said to him, "go, if you think duty calls you." He came into the city—where many thirsted for his blood—because after asking counsel of God daily, he was strengthened in his convictions that for him to give way would be a base desertion of his post. He wrote: "I was alone in St. Louis, with none but God of whom to ask counsel. But, thrice blessed be his name, he did not forsake me. I was enabled, deliberately and unreservedly, to surrender myself to him. I thought of mother, of brothers and sisters, and above all, of my dearest wife, and felt that I could give them all up for Jesus' sake.　I think I could have gone to the stake and not a nerve have trembled, nor a lip quivered.　Under the influence of these feelings, I wrote and sent forth my appeal."

It will be noticed that his "Appeal to Fellow-Citizens" was made in a spirit of the utmost kindness.　There is not the slightest indication of a fanatic therein.　He could no more have been true to his deepest convictions and at the same time have avoided St. Louis, than could have Martin Luther have avoided Worms, when he declared he would go there even "though he should find as many devils as there are tiles upon the house-top."　This same gentle but decided spirit has always characterized the Christian martyr.　It was strikingly manifested by one of Cromwell's common soldiers, who published a remarkable tract during the captivity of Charles the First.　From this tract Coleridge has copied the following noble sentiments, which accord well with those which Mr. Lovejoy entertained:

"I judge it ten times more honorable for a single person in witnessing a truth to oppose the world in its power, wisdom, and authority—this standing in its full strength and he singly and nakedly—than fighting many battles by force of arms and gaining them all　I have no life but truth; and if truth be advanced by my suffering, then my life also.　If truth live, I live; and these can not die, but by any man suffering for them are enlarged, enthroned. Death can not hurt me.　I sport with him, am above his reach."—(*The Friend, Essay 1st.*)

We can now see what a mistake was committed, when citizens of Boston and St. Louis, as well as of other cities, supposed it possible to stifle free speech.

The martyr-spirit of Christ was still enthroned in many breasts and could not be cast out by persecution.

LETTER FROM COL. GEO. T. M. DAVIS, OF NEW YORK.

Col. Geo. T. M. Davis, who resided at Alton, in 1837, has handed me the following account of a little incident illustrating the fearless bravery of Mr. Lovejoy:

"There is no incident in the life of E. P. Lovejoy that revealed in brighter hues the moral grandeur of his character, and his fearless devotion to principle, than the following:

"A few weeks prior to the assembling of the mob on the 7th of November, 1837,—in the resistance of whose attack upon Mr. Gilman's building, as well as upon his own life and that of others associated with him, he met his death,— some eight or ten citizens of Alton, calling themselves of the highest respectability, determined to tar and feather Mr. Lovejoy, and then send him adrift, in a canoe secured for such purpose, down the Mississippi River. The night selected for the consummation of their designs was as bright and clear as could be. Mr. Lovejoy resided at the time at Hunterstown, in a building in a secluded spot below the road that led to Upper-Alton, and his wife, whom he idolized, was prostrated upon a bed of sickness, with but little hope of her physicians or husband that she could ever recover. Between ten and eleven o'clock, while on his way on foot to the drug-store in Alton, a distance of about three-quarters of a mile from his residence, to procure some medicine for his wife, he was met by these eight or ten citizens,—all of them disguised,—who stopped him in the road, and at once disclosed to him their object and purpose. With the most perfect composure and calmness, he immediately replied to them: 'Gentlemen, I have but a single request to make of you. My wife is dangerously ill, and it is necessary she should have this prescription immediately, and which I was on the way to town to procure. Will one of you take it and see that it is delivered at the house, but without intimating what is about to befall me. I am in the hands of God, and am ready to go with you.'

"For a few moments, entire silence reigned. At last it was broken by one of the medical men that made up in part the disguised party, exclaiming: 'Boys, I can't lay my hand upon as brave a man as this is,' and turning away, was followed by the rest, and Mr. Lovejoy was spared the degredation of being tarred and feathered, though, a few weeks later, he suffered the death of a martyr, in the defence of the liberty of the press and of speech.

"It is a most singular coincidence, that scarcely one of those who made up the tar-and-feathering party of that night, died a natural death. And, it is still more singular, that the one who refused to lay violent hands upon him and who saved Mr. Lovejoy at the time, was a Southern man."

CHAPTER IX.

Lovejoy requested to retire from the editorial chair of the "Observer"—The paper sold—He is called back again—His comments on the burning of a negro in St. Louis—On a charge of Judge Lawless to the Grand Jury.

The effects of Mr. Lovejoy's noble utterances were "tremendous," as he wrote to his brother.

The original proprietors of the *Observer* waited on him and requested him to retire from the editorial chair. For two days the result seemed altogether doubtful, but then the tide began to turn, and even some who were not in sympathy with the religious views of the paper said, "the *Observer* must be sustained or our liberties are gone." He wrote to his brother at that time as follows: "The pressure, which seemed as though it would crush me to the earth, began to lighten. Light began to break in upon the gloomiest day I have ever seen. I can not think or write about it without my eyes filling with tears, to think of the deliverance which God wrought by so weak and unworthy an instrument as I am."

He cheerfully consented to give up editing the *Observer*, at the request of the original proprietors, and thought that his work and responsibility were ended. But such was not the issue. The paper was in debt, and the proprietors,—glad to get rid of the elephant on their hands,—gave up the press and materials to a Mr. Moore, the endorser on a note, soon to fall due. This gentleman in-

73

sisted on Lovejoy's continuance as editor, with the single condition that the paper should be removed to Alton, Illinois.

The citizens of Alton were cordial,—"received him with open arms,"—but while arrangements were being considered for the removal, Lovejoy received a letter signed by Mr. Moore and others, abjuring him, "by all means," to come back. In consequence of that letter, the project of removing the press to Alton was, at that time, abandoned. His enemies, discovering that he could not be frightened, and that his "appeal" had rallied around him a few friends, concluded it wisest to let him alone. A period of comparative quiet ensued, but this was only the calm before another storm.

ARTICLE ON THE BURNING OF A NEGRO AT THE STAKE, IN ST. LOUIS.

In the *Observer*, of May 5th, 1836, the following article appeared in the editorial columns:

"AWFUL MURDER AND SAVAGE BARBARITY.

"The transactions we are about to relate, took place on Thursday, a week ago, and even yet we have not recovered from the shock they gave us. Our hand trembles as we record the story. The following are the particulars, as nearly as we have been able to ascertain them from the city papers, and from the relation of those who were eye-and-ear witnesses of the termination of the awful scene:

"On the afternoon of Thursday, the 28th ult., an affray between two sailors, or boatmen, took place on the steamboat landing. Mr. George Hammond, deputy sheriff, and Mr. William Mull, deputy constable, in the discharge of their official duty, attempted to arrest the boatmen for a breach of the peace. In so doing they were set upon by a mulatto fellow, by the name of Francis J. McIntosh, who had just arrived in the city, as cook, on board the steamboat "Flora," from Pittsburgh. In consequence the boatmen escaped, and McIntosh was arrested for his interference with the officers. He was carried before Patrick Walsh, Esq., a justice of the peace for this county, and by him committed to jail, and delivered to the same officers to be taken thither.

"On his way, he inquired what his punishment would be, and being told that it would not be less than five years' imprisonment in the State Prison, he immediately broke loose from the officers, drew a long knife and made a desperate blow at Mr. Mull, but fortunately missed him.

"Unfortunately, however, a second blow, aimed with the same savage violence, had better success, and struck Mr. Mull in the right side, and wounded him severely. He was then seized by the shoulder, by Mr. Hammond, whereat he turned and stabbed him in the neck. The knife struck the lower part of the chin and passed deeply into the neck, cutting the jugular vein and the larger arteries. Mr. H. turned from his murderer, walked about sixty steps, fell and expired! Mr. M., although dangerously wounded, was able to pursue the murderer who had fled, until his cries alarmed the people in the vicinity. They turned out, and without much difficulty secured the bloodthirsty wretch and lodged him in jail.

"The bloody deeds of which McIntosh had been guilty soon became known through the city; and crowds col-

lected at the spot where the body of Mr. Hammond lay
weltering in its blood.   The excitement was intense, and
soon might be heard above the tumult, the voices of a few
exhorting the multitude to take summary vengeance.   The
plan and process of proceeding were soon resolved on.   A
mob was immediately organized and went forward to the
jail in search of their victim.   The sheriff, Mr. Brotherton,
made some attempts to oppose their illegal violence.   Ap-
prehensive for the fate of his family, who occupied a
portion of the jail building, he then retired, taking them
along with him, to a place of safety.   Another of our fellow-citizens courageously attempted to reason with the
angry mob, and to stay them from their fearful proceedings.   When, however, 'he saw that he could prevail
nothing, but that rather a tumult was made,' being himself
threatened with violence, he was compelled to retire from
the place and leave the enraged multitude to do their work.

"All was done with the utmost deliberation and system,
and an awful stillness pervaded the scene, broken only by
the sound of the implements employed in demolishing the
prison doors.   Those who have read Scott's description of
the Porteous mob, as given in the 'Heart of Mid-Lothian,'
will have an accurate idea of the manner of proceeding at
the jail, on Thursday night.

"All was still; men spoke to each other in whispers,
but it was a whisper which made the blood curdle to hear
it, and indicated the awful energy of purpose with which
they were bent upon sacrificing the life of their intended
victim.   Armed persons were stationed as guards to protect those engaged in breaking down the doors.

"At length, between eight and nine o'clock at night, the cell of the wretch was reached. Loud shouts of execration and triumph rent the air as he was dragged forth and hurried away to the scene of the burnt sacrifice! Some seized him by the hair, some by the arms and legs, and in this way he was carried to a large locust tree in the rear of the town, not far from the jail. He was then chained to the tree with his back against its trunk, and facing to the south. The wood, consisting of rails, plank, etc., was then piled up before him, about as high as his knees, shavings and a brand were brought, and the fire kindled!

"Up to this time, as we are informed, McIntosh uttered not a word; but when the fire had seized upon its victim, he begged that some one in the crowd would shoot him. He then commenced singing a hymn and trying to pray. Afterwards he hung his head and suffered in silence, until roused by some one saying that he must be already out of his misery. Upon this, though wrapped in flames, and though the fire had obliterated the features of humanity, he raised his head and spoke out distinctly, saying: 'No, no: I feel as much as any of you, I hear you all; shoot me, shoot me.' He was burning about twenty minutes before life became extinct.

"But the tale of depravity and woe is not yet all told. After the crowd had somewhat dispersed, a rabble of boys, who had attended to witness the horrid rites, commenced amusing themselves by throwing stones at the black and disfigured corpse, as it stood chained to the tree. The object was to see who should first succeed in breaking the skull!

"Such, according to the best information we have been able to obtain, is a faithful description of the scene that has been transacted in our midst. It has given us pain to record it; but, in doing so, we feel, deeply feel, that we are fulfilling a solemn duty which, as one of its members, we owe to this community, and as an American citizen, to our country at large. Let no one suppose that we would lightly say a word in derogation of the character of the city in which we live; on the contrary, we have, as is natural, a strong desire to sustain and vindicate its reputation. But when constitutional law and order are at stake, when the question lies between justice regularly administered, or the wild vengeance of a mob, then there is but one side on which the patriot and the Christian can rally; but one course for them to pursue.

"We have drawn the above gloomy and hideous picture, not for the purpose of holding it up as a fair representation of the moral condition of St. Louis,—for we loudly protest against any such conclusion, and we call upon our fellow-citizens to join us in such protest,—but that the immediate actors in the horrid tragedy may see the work of their hands, and shrink in horror from a repetition of it, and in humble penitence seek forgiveness of that community whose laws they have so outraged, and of that God whose image they have, without his permission, wickedly defaced; and that we may all see (and be warned in time) the legitimate result of the spirit of mobism, and whither, unless arrested in its first out-breakings, it is sure to carry us. In Charlestown, it burns a convent over the head of defenceless women; in Baltimore, it desecrates the

Sabbath, and works all that day in demolishing a private
citizen's house; in Vicksburg, it hangs up gamblers, three
or four in a row; and, in St. Louis, it forces a man—a
hardened wretch certainly, and one that deserved to die,
but not *thus* to die—it forces him from beneath the ægis
of our constitution and laws, hurries him to the stake and
burns him alive!

"It is not yet five years since the first mob, within the
memory of man (for the French settlers of this city were
a peaceable people, and their descendants continue so),
was organized in St. Louis. They commenced operations
by tearing down the brothels of the city; and the good
citizens of the place, not aware of the danger, and in consideration of the good done, aside from the manner of
doing it, rather sanctioned the proceeding, at least, they
did not condemn it. The next thing was to burn our Governor in effigy, because in the discharge of one of the most
solemn functions belonging to his official character, he
had not acted in accordance with the public sentiment of
a part of this community. The next achievement was to
tear down a gambling-house; and this was done last
winter. The next and last we need not again repeat.

"And now we make our appeal to the citizens of this
community, and wherever else our voice can be heard, and
ask, and ask with the most heart-felt anxiety, is it not
time to stop? We know that in a case like the present, it
is difficult to withdraw our thoughts and feelings from the
great provocation to violence, to be found in the murderous atrocity of the wretch who has so fearfully atoned for
his crime. But we do say, and insist, that these considera-

tions must not be permitted to enter at all, into our reasoning and practice on this point. We *must* stand by the constitution and laws, or all is gone!

"For ourselves, we do not hesitate to say that we have awful forebodings on this subject. Not of St. Louis in particular, for the experience of the past year has shown that we are 'not sinners above other' cities,—but for our whole country.

"We have, as a nation, violated God's holy Sabbath, profaned His holy name, and given ourselves up to covetousness, licentiousness, and every evil work; and He in return seems evidently to be withdrawing the influences of His spirit from the land, and leaving us to be 'filled with our own devices.' And the consequences are plainly to be seen. Men and communities, hitherto peaceable and orderly, are breaking over all restraints of law and shame, and deeds are done amongst us which show that man is yet a fiend at heart.

"We visited the scene of the burning, on the day following, about noon. We stood and gazed for a moment or two upon the blackened and mutilated trunk—for that was all which remained—of McIntosh before us, and as we turned away, in bitterness of heart, we prayed that we might not live. The prayer, and perhaps the feeling which dictated it, might be wrong, yet still, after a week's reflection, our heart will still repeat it. For so fearful are our anticipations of the calamities that are to come upon this nation (and which, unless averted by a speedy and thorough repentance, we have no more doubt will fall upon us, than we have that a God of holiness and justice is our

supreme governor), that were our work done, and were it
His will, we would gladly be 'taken away from the evil to
come.'   Meantime, let every Christian, and especially
every minister of the sanctuary, flee to a throne of grace,
and standing between the porch and the altar, weeping,
pray:—'Spare thy people, oh Lord, and give not thy heri-
tage to reproach.'"

LOVEJOY'S SEVERE EDITORIAL COMMENTS ON THE
CHARGE OF JUDGE LAWLESS.

In the summer of 1836, there was a certain Judge Lawless on the bench at St. Louis.   It became his duty to
charge the grand jury in the matter of the burning of the
negro McIntosh.   Strange coincidence between name and
character!   Like Mr. Byends, in the "Pilgrim's Progress,"
this foggy-minded gentleman had "the luck of jumping in
his judgment with the present way of the times."   A mob
had been sanctioned by "most respectable citizens" when
they whipped white men who were "suspected" of enticing
away slaves.   Now, the Judge would not disapprove the
act when the offence was the burning of a negro.   In this
charge the ground is openly taken that a crime which, if
committed by one or two, would be punishable with death,
may be perpetrated by the multitude with impunity.   Says
the Judge:—"If, on the other hand, the destruction of the
murderer of Hammond was the act, as I have said, of the
many,—of the multitude, in the ordinary sense of these
words,—not the act of numerable and ascertainable male-
factors, but of congregated thousands, seized upon and
impelled by that mysterious, metaphysical, and almost

electric frenzy, which, in all ages and nations, has hurried on the infuriated multitude to deeds of death and destruction,—then, I say, act not at all in the matter; the case then transcends your jurisdiction—it is beyond the reach of human law."

Commenting on this charge, Mr. Lovejoy wrote, under date July 21, 1836:

"1. In this charge of Judge Lawless we see exemplified and illustrated the truth of the doctrine we have, for years, been endeavoring to impress on the minds of our countrymen, viz.: That foreigners educated in the old world never can come to have a proper understanding of American constitutional law. Judge Lawless is a foreigner,—a naturalized one it is true, but still to all intents and purposes a foreigner,—he was educated and received his notions of government amidst the turbulent agitations of Ireland, and, at a period, too, when anarchy and illegal violence prevailed to a degree unprecedented even in the annals of that wretched and most unhappy land. Amidst the lawless and violent proceedings of those times Mr. Lawless grew up. He is next found in arms, in the service of France, fighting against the country to whom his allegiance was due. His third appearance, in a public capacity, is as judge in one of the Republican States of America, where he delivers such a charge to our grand jury as the one now under our consideration.

"We disclaim all wish or intention to wound the feelings, or injure the personal reputation, of Judge Lawless; but we do wish to disarm the monstrous doctrines he has promulgated from the bench, of their power, either as a present rule, or a future precedent; and we apprehend that when the school, in which the Judge was educated, is known and candidly considered, his notions of practical justice, at once so novel to Americans, so absurd and so wicked, will have little influence with our sound-hearted, home-educated Republicans.

"2. Judge Lawless is a Papist; and in his charge we see the cloven foot of Jesuitism peeping out from under the veil of almost every paragraph in the charge. What is Jesuitism but another name for the doctrine that principles ought to change according to circumstances? and this is the very identical doctrine of the charge. A horrid crime must not be punished because, forsooth, it would be difficult perhaps to do it. The principles of justice and of constitutional law, must yield to a doubtful question of present expediency. Doubtless the Judge is not aware whence he derived these notions; and yet it cannot be doubted that they came originally from St. Omers, where so many Irish priests are educated. So true is it, that Popery in its very essential principles is incompatible with regulated, civil, or religious liberty. Our warning voice on this subject is lifted up in vain; but some of those who now hear it, will live to mourn over their present incredulity and indifference.

"3. In his answer to the remarks of the New York *American*, Judge Lawless intimates that the safety of this office is owing to the course he took in this matter. We do not believe him; but, if he says true, then what a disgraceful truth to St. Louis! What had the *Observer* done? It had told the story of the horrid tragedy enacted here in plain, unvarnished terms, just as the affair occurred. No one pretends that our version of the affair was incorrect, and we added nothing more than in the spirit of earnest and solemn warning, to entreat our fellow-citizens to stay such proceedings, or their all was lost. And for this the Judge says, but for his interposition, our office would have been destroyed. That is, a mob in St. Louis burns a man up, and then citizens tear down the office of the press that dares to reprobate such an act. This assertion of the Judge is a gross libel upon the city, as we verily believe. We have never heard of any threats to pull down our office, which did not originate with his countrymen. Mark that?

"But even supposing it true, and that our office was endangered by what we wrote concerning the McIntosh tragedy, we desire no such volunteers as Judge Lawless, with such principles, to come to our rescue. We reject all such. We desire not to be saved at such an expense. To establish our institutions of civil and religious liberty, to obtain freedom of opinion and of the press, guaranteed by constitutional law, cost thousands, yea, tens of thousands of valuable lives. And let them not be parted with, at least, for less than cost.

"We covet not the loss of property, nor the honors of martyrdom; but better, far better, that the office of the *Observer* should be scattered in fragments to the four winds of heaven; yea, better that editor, printer, and publishers should be chained to the same tree as McIntosh, and share his fate, than that the doctrines promulgated by Judge Lawless, from the bench, should become prevalent in this community. For they are subversive of all law, and at once open the door for the perpetration, by a congregated mob, calling themselves the people, of every species of violence, and that, too, with perfect impunity.

"Society is resolved into its first elements, and every man must hold his property and his life at the point of the dagger.

"Having traveled somewhat extensively of late, we have had opportunity of learning the impression made abroad by recent occurrences in this city. And we know that the feeling, excited by this charge of Judge Lawless, is far more unfavorable than that consequent upon the burning of McIntosh.

"'For that,' say they, 'was the act of an excited mob, but here is the Judge on his bench, in effect sanctioning it!'

"The subject grows upon our hands, but we forbear. We again repeat that we have had no wish, in all we have said, to injure the reputation of Judge Lawless. The subject is one altogether too important to allow personal feelings to enter into the discussion of it, either one way or the other. For all that part of his charge, where an attempt is made to identify the *Observer* with Abolitionism, and then charge upon that the McIntosh tragedy, we can only say, that we have not the least doubt that the Judge is perfectly sincere in the expression of this opinion. And the ignorance and prejudice which could lead to such an expression of opinion, however censurable in the Judge, is still more pitiable in the man. Of this part of the charge, Charles Hammond, of the *Cincinnati Gazette*, says: 'It is as fanatical as the highest state of Abolition fanaticism can be.'"

CHAPTER X.

The *St. Louis Observer* of June 21, 1836, which contained the foregoing severe criticism of Judge Lawless' charge to the grand jury, announced Mr. Lovejoy's intention to remove the paper to the then rapidly growing city of Alton, in Illinois. This decision was made on pecuniary grounds chiefly, and not for personal consideration. The "new code" had become more popular in St. Louis since the day when the two white men had been whipped one hundred to two hundred lashes each, by "most respectable citizens." Now a Judge "had bid the law make courtesy to their will," in his charge to the grand jury. It was only necessary for them now to fancy that they were "seized upon and impelled by a mysterious, metaphysical, and almost electric frenzy," in order to elevate their united action 'into a region far above the "jurisdiction of the grand jury." This was a most comforting doctrine; "Hooking both right and wrong to the appetite, to follow as it draws." The way, therefore, was made easy to put the "new code" in practice, and the time for doing so in the case of the *St. Louis Observer* was short.

In a few days the press, the type, and the editor's furniture were to be shipped to Alton. The "respectable citizens" must be quick. The *Observer* office was, therefore, entered at St. Louis, and much of the property—including part of the editor's furniture—was destroyed and cast into the Mississippi River. What was left of the press was shipped to Alton, and the editor, with his little family, followed after.

At this period, the subject of the scrupulous observance of Sunday, as holy time, was receiving especial and very unusual attention. Many Christian merchants in the West refused either to travel upon steamboats or to receive freight from them on that day. Unfortunately the remains of Mr. Lovejoy's St. Louis printing press arrived at Alton, and was discharged upon the river bank before daylight on Sunday morning. It remained all day, for the inspection of the vulgar crowd, and before the next morning, it was destroyed and cast into the Mississippi River!

This act was immediately disavowed at a public meeting by the citizens of Alton, and money was raised to supply a new press. Mr. Lovejoy was still in favor of gradual emancipation, and at that meeting he avowed himself "the uncompromising enemy of slavery," though not an Abolitionist. Ten of the most respectable citizens* of Alton testified subsequently that he closed his remarks as follow: "But, gentlemen, as long as I am an American citizen, and as long as American blood runs in these veins, I shall hold

* The names of these gentlemen, two or three of whom I believe are still living, are: Geo. Walworth, A. B. Roff, Solomon E. Moore, Effingham Cock, John W. Chickering, James Morse, jr., F. W. Graves, W. L. Chappell, J. H. Alexander, Chas. W. Hunter.

myself at libery to speak, to write, and to publish whatever
I please on any subject, being amenable to the laws of my
country for the same."

This testimony, certifying what Lovejoy said, was given
by these gentlemen in consequence of the circulation of a
false report that, at the meeting above referred to, he had
pledged himself not to discuss the subject of slavery. No
candid person, who has read the statements embodied in
this book, can for a moment believe that Elijah P. Lovejoy
ever could have made a pledge of that sort.

Lovejoy's new press soon arrived, and on September 8,
1836, the first number of the *Alton Observer* was issued.
It continued to be issued regularly until August 17, 1837,
soon after which it again became the object of mob violence.
During this period of comparative quiet, Lovejoy took the
same bold, uncompromising stand against slavery and corruption, yet treating all opponents fairly and kindly.

CHAPTER XI.

Lovejoy's letters and editorial articles at this time—His heroic
wife—His view of Slavery—The cry of Amalgamation—
The right application of the Gospel—The doctrines of
anti-slavery men.

In the sickly summer of 1836, Lovejoy and his delicate
wife both suffered so much that, at times, his trials seemed
everpowering. The following extract is from a letter
dated August 31, 1836, to his mother: "Why, when my
services are so much needed, I shall be laid up on a bed of
sickness, I can not tell; why, when God has, in his wise and
holy providence, let loose upon me angry and wicked men,
he should also so heavily lay his own hand upon me, I
can not see, but he can, and I desire to submit without a
murmur. I can now *feel*, as I never felt before, the wisdom of Paul's advice not to marry; and yet I would not
be without the consolations which my dear wife and child
afford me for all the world. Still I can not but feel that it
is harder to 'fight valiantly' for the truth, when I risk not
only my own comfort, ease, and reputation, and even life, but
also that of another beloved one. But in this I am greatly
favored. My dear wife is a perfect heroine. Though of
delicate health, she endures affliction more calmly than I
had supposed possible for a woman to do. Never has
she, by a single word, attempted to turn me from the
scene of warfare and danger; never has she whispered a
feeling of discontent at the hardships to which she has

been subjected in consequence of her marriage to me, and those have been neither few nor small, and some of them peculiarly calculated to wound the sensibility of a woman. She has seen me shunned, hated, and reviled, by those who were once my dearest friends; she has heard the execrations wide and deep upon my head, and she has only clung to me the more closely and more devotedly. When I told her that the mob had destroyed a considerable portion of our furniture, along with their other depredations, 'No matter,' said she, 'what they have destroyed since they have not hurt you.' Such is woman! and such is the woman whom God has given me.* And now do you ask, are you discouraged? I answer promptly, no. I have opened my mouth for the dumb, I have plead the cause of the poor and oppressed, I have maintained the rights of humanity, and of nature outraged in the person of my fellow-men around me, and I have done it, as is my nature, openly, boldly, and in the face of day, and for these things I am brought into these straits. For these things I have seen my family scattered, my office broken up, my furniture—as I was moving it to this place—destroyed; have been loaded with execrations, had all manner of evil spoken of me falsely, and finally, had my life threatened,

---

* Her maiden name was Celia Ann French, and her former residence was St. Charles, Missouri. She was a fragile and beautiful girl of 21, when he married her in 1835. She died some years since, without ever having entirely recovered from the trials of 1837. Before her death, she became quite poor, passed several days at my house, a broken-down, prematurely-old person, possessed of scarce a trace of her early beauty. The prophecy regarding her, made in 1837, that "her strong heart would break down her physical frame," was, indeed, most sadly verified.   H. T.

and laid down at night, weary and sick, with the expectation that I might be aroused by the stealthy step of the
assassin. This was the case the last night I spent at St.
Louis. Yet none of these things move me from my purpose; by the grace of God I will not, I will not forsake my
principles; and I will maintain and propagate them with
all the means he puts into my hands. The cry of the
oppressed has entered not only into my ears but into my
soul, so that while I live I can not hold my peace."

HIS VIEW OF SLAVERY.

In a letter to the *Christian Mirror*, dated Alton, February 9, 1837, Mr. Lovejoy expressed profound regret that
several of the most prominent religious newspapers were
then sending to their hundred thousand readers "partial
and injurious representations of the character and motives
of those engaged in freeing the slave from bondage, while
their columns were hermetically sealed to all reply or con-
futation." He added: "If the wisdom of the schools can
not teach you the true character of slavery, come with me,
and let us interrogate yonder illiterate, untaught slave.
He is just returning, faint and weary, from the toils of the
day. He is an aged man, and has had, for many years, a
practical acquaintance with slavery. Let us hear his reply
to the question, 'What is Slavery?' 'It is to have my
back subjected to the cowhide, or the cart-whip, at the will
or caprice of my master, or any of his family. Every
child has a right to curse, or kick, or cuff the old man. It
is to toil all day beneath an almost vertical sun, with the
bitter certainty always before me, that not one cent of
what I earn is, or can be, my own. It is to depart from

my hut every morning with the sickening fear, that before I return at night, it will be visited by the slave-driving fiend. It is to return at night, and find my worst fears realized. My first-born son, denied even the poor privilege of bidding his father farewell, is on his way, a chained and manacled victim, to a distant market, there to be disposed of in shambles, where human flesh and sinews are bought and sold. It is to enter my cabin, and see my wife or daughter struggling in the lustful embraces of my master, or some of his white friends, without daring to attempt their rescue; for should I open my lips to remonstrate, a hundred lashes would be the consequence; and should I raise my hand to smite the brutal wretch, nothing but death could atone for the sacrilege. But above all, to be a slave, is to be denied the privilege of reading the gospel of the Son of God, to have no control over my own children, and, consequently to be deprived of the power and means of educating them in the principles of morality and religion. In one word, it is to be degraded from a man to a brute,—to become, instead of a free moral agent, a thing, a piece of property, and to be used as such—to be deprived of all personal and all civil rights—to be shut out from all enjoyment in this world, and all hope in the next.' Such, brother Cummings, is slavery; not that slavery such as you may imagine or hope might exist, but slavery as it actually now exists in eleven of these United States, nay, such as it exists in the church."

THE CRY OF "AMALGAMATION."

The *Baptist Banner*, published in 1837, at Louisville, Kentucky, charged the Abolitionists with the advocacy of intermarriage between whites and blacks!—"the union of persons that God by color, has put asunder, as much as He has separated midnight from noonday." Mr. Lovejoy answered his brother editor as follows: (It was believed that facts fully justified the illustration of amalgamation to which Mr. Lovejoy alluded.)

"The Abolitionists are beginning every where to throw off the mask, and boldly to advocate amalgamation; that is, the intermarriage of whites and blacks!—the union of persons that God by color, has put asunder, as much as he has separated midnight from noonday!"—*Baptist Banner*.

"Now, brother, of the *Banner*, stop a moment, and do not go off at half-charge, as you are somewhat apt to do. Let us reason together a moment,—only for a moment.

"In the first place, we ask you for the proof of the above statement. We deny its truth. We read most of the Abolition publications in the land, and we have never seen any such position taken by any one of them. Bring forward your proof, therefore, or acknowledge yourself mistaken, and that you have borne false witness against your neighbor.

"But secondly, if God has put the black and white races so far asunder, how happens it that they come together so readily in the State where you live? Is not the Vice-President of these United States, and one of your own citizens, an 'amalgamator,' as you phrase it? Are not his 'amalgamated' daughters among you, respectably married to men of pure Saxon blood—the sons of chivalrous Kentucky?

"Moreover, go out into the streets of Louisville, the

city of your residence, and where there are no Abolitionists, and tell me how many individuals among all the
colored population that throng your streets, you can find
whose faces shine with the pure gloss of an African complexion.   Such persons are about as scarce in St. Louis as
black swans are on the Mississippi, and we suspect the
case is pretty similar in Louisville.

"Now, if this amalgamation *must* go on—certainly the
taste of those individuals who practically favor it, is widely
different from ours, but you know the old proverb, brother,
De gustibus, etc.—if, then, it must go on, had it not better
be so regulated as that it shall, in future, be in accordance
with the divine as well as human law, rather than, as now,
in contravention to both?

"If, for instance, an individual in Kentucky, like your
illustrious citizen, the Vice-President, should prefer the
daughters of Ham rather than the daughters of Japheth,
from whom to choose a wife, why should we who prefer
the latter be restricted to one, while he is allowed a dozen,
and indeed a whole harem, if he please ?   And why, when
we are bound to love, cherish, and maintain our wives till
death, should he be allowed the privilege of making
'merchandise' of his, and their children too, just as caprice
or avarice may dictate?

"Will the *Banner* answer these questions satisfactorily,
if he can, to his own conscience; and if he can not, 'be
ashamed and confounded, and never open his mouth more'
about the 'amalgamation' of Abolitionists?"

THE RIGHT APPLICATION OF THE GOSPEL.

Lovejoy was once opposed to the discussion of slavery!

In 1835, he had advanced to the position of a colonizationist, and favored the gradual emancipation of the slaves.
Now, in 1837, he had further changed, and had come into
sympathy with immediate Abolition.

Does the reader judge he was unstable? He was one
of the stablest of men; but he possessed also the qualities
which have been claimed to be the most fruitful gifts of
genius,—"openness and simplicity of mind, a readiness to
entertain and a willingness to accept, and enthusiastically
to pursue, a new idea."

It was because of his superiority, therefore, that his
opinions grew, and this raised him above all fear of the
charge of inconsistency. He now believed that the cor-
rupt tree could not possibly be made to produce good
fruit, and that the gospel must be applied to cut it down
at the roots rather than to lop off the branches.

The following article on the subject of the "Right Remedy," was published at Alton, March 16, 1837:

"We frequently hear from many good brethren the remark, that whatever may be the evils of slavery, the way
to remedy them, is 'to preach the gospel.' In opposition
to efforts made by anti-slavery societies, and anti-slavery
presses, they say: 'If the gospel will not effect it (the
abolition of slavery), we despair of any instrumentality
whatever.'

"We would respectfully ask these brethren, what they
mean by such remarks as these? We agree with them
most cordially, that the gospel of the Son of God is the
remedy for slavery. But how? They certainly will not
say, that it will prove this remedy as administered by

those, their ministerial brethren, who maintain that the bible sanctions slavery, makes it right, and places it on the same footing, in its code of morals, as the domestic relations of husband and wife, parent and child? Not in such hands will the gospel prove a remedy for the evils of slavery.

"But how much more good can it effect, when used by those who, notwithstanding they admit the remedy to be a good one, uniformly decline applying it, for fear of irritating their patients?

"How long will it take the gospel to work a cure, if it is never applied to the diseased part? Will these brethren tell us? They seem to imagine there is some magic power about the preaching of the gospel, that is to do away with slavery, while yet the authorized and accredited ministers of the gospel never open their lips to delare that slavery is condemned by it. If they do not mean this, we should be glad to know what it is they mean, by their constantly repeating 'the gospel is the remedy, the gospel is the remedy'; while as yet they are as constantly condemning the conduct of those who seek to make it the remedy indeed, by proclaiming it to be, in all its principles and precèpts, opposed to slavery.

"The Rev. James Douglass, whom we have known, and whom we highly respect as a devoted servant of Christ, in a communication to the *Boston Recorder*, which other eastern papers are copying, has much of this *indefiniteness* of view about the gospel proving a remedy for slavery. He would have anti-slavery men, instead of persisting in their present efforts to abolish slavery, send ministers to the

South, to 'preach the gospel,' to both masters and slaves. 'For,' says he, 'where religion flourishes, slaves are well-treated.' Aye, there's the very point. And this, then, is all the gospel, as preached at the South, is able or expected to effect—the good treatment of the slave. Now, we wish to aid in the preaching of no 'gospel' whose ultimate aim, as it respects the slaves, goes no farther than this. The 'gospel of the Son of God' requires not the 'good treatment' of the black man as a *slave*, but as a man, and a moral and accountable being; and the very first step in this good treatment is to SET HIM FREE. Take an illustration of our meaning:

"When the apostle Paul went out into the Gentile world to 'preach the gospel,' he found his hearers all idolaters. He moreover found that in the practice of this idolatry, the most shameful rites abounded. The heathen of both sexes were accustomed to spend their nights in the temples of their idols, in promiscuous, and most disgusting licentiousness. Now, suppose he had commenced preaching the gospel to these polluted idolaters in this way: 'I will not, oh men of Athens and Corinth, require too much of you at once. I will say nothing of the divine honors you pay to Jupiter, and Mars, and Mercury, and Venus, and your other innumerable gods and goddesses; but I do require, in the name of my Master, that, when you worship these deities, and especially the latter, you should do it in a little more respectable and decent manner. If you will cease these, your midnight orgies in the temples of your gods, and prosecute their worship no farther than to offer them daily libations, and to prostrate yourselves before their images, it is, I think, all the gospel requires of you at present. And for the rest, if indeed this be not sufficient, I leave you to learn it from my successor, Timothy.' And thus had the apostle Paul understood the 'preaching of the gospel,' as many of his modern successors seem to do, Christ would have died, not to *abolish* idolatry, but to 'remedy its evils,' and thus make it respectable! At least, this could have been the only result for two or three centuries after his departure from the world. If it be said that because we can not abolish slavery at once, that is no good reason why we should not rejoice to see, and, as far as in us lies, endeavor to effect the amelioration of the condition of slaves, as slaves, we admit the correctness of the remark. When Paul was preaching the gospel to the Gentiles, he would undoubtedly be glad to see the heathen quitting their licentious practices, even though they did not go so far as to abandon their idols. This was so much good effected; and so we are glad to see slave-holders treating their slaves with kindness, teaching them to read the Bible (which, however, they hardly ever do), sending them to the Sabbath-school and the church. But what we are protesting against, is the idea that the gospel is satisfied and its precepts fulfilled, when these things, and only these, are done. If you rob a man of ten dollars, it is better you should spend the money in disseminating copies of the bible, than of 'Tom Paine's Age of Reason'; but doing the former will no more justify the original theft than the latter. The gospel has no method of teaching the robber how to dispose of the avails of his violence, so that he may retain them without sin. It has, and can have, but one precept in the case,—'Restore what thou hast wickedly taken.' So, if the gospel is to be preached to the masters of slaves, all it can say is, 'Restore the slave to himself; give him back those rights which belong to him, as he is man, and which can not be taken away, without robbing both him and his God.'"

CHAPTER XII.

The beginning of the end—The summer of 1837—Petitions for
the abolition of Slavery in the District of Columbia—Call
for the formation of the Illinois Anti-Slavery Society—Lovejoy's most obnoxious editorial article.

I have now brought the reader to a point in the mid-
summer of 1837, when men's brains were at fever heat on
the subject of slavery—to a period only about four months
prior to the end of our hero's life-work!   At that time, the
great State of Illinois contained only about four hundred
thousand inhabitants!   Chicago was estimated at less than
four thousand! and Alton, not far from the same number.
The inhabitants of this latter city were not only prodig-
iously enterprising, expecting it to become a metropolis,
but were foremost in furthering all moral and religious
reforms.

From New York, they had drawn Timothy Turner, then
as effective a temperance lecturer as could be found.   They
were sending forth through the West each month about
six thousand copies of the *Illinois Temperance Herald,* a
large newspaper filled with stimulating thought promotive
of that cause, and at further large expense, they had induced A. W. Corey* to settle at Alton and become its
editor.

* A. W. Corey, whilst editor of the *Temperance Herald,* provoked heated
opposition in St. Louis, by his bold denunciation of the liquor traffic.   At
one time, after a scathing article on this subject, he published the names of all
the wholesale grocers at St. Louis, who sold liquors, charging them with par-

Revivals of religion were so universal about that time, that many, in their fervent zeal, expected the dawn of the millennium was at hand.   Great preachers were attracted to Illinois, among them, the celebrated Gideon Blackburn, of Kentucky; James Gallagher, from Tennessee, and many others.   Ten young divinity students at Yale College banded together to settle in Illinois, with high hopes of eminent usefulness.   The late Rev. Theron Baldwin, well known both East and West, was one of these.

A missionary spirit pervaded the minds of thousands in the State.   In the East, the excitement was quite as great on moral subjects.

William Lloyd Garrison had faced the bitter opposition of the sympathizers with the South, and had partially triumphed over the attempts made to silence his voice.

He had been mobbed, put in prison, and dragged through the streets of Boston with a rope around his body!   Five thousand dollars reward was offered by the Legislature of Georgia for his conviction under law.

John Quincy Adams, late President of the United States,

ticipating in a common crime.   Many, in their fury, would have been glad to have wiped out of existence not only the *Observer*, but also the *Temperance Herald*, with their editors, printers, and offices, as nuisances in society.   Both Turner and Corey afterwards settled at Godfrey, Ill., four miles north of Alton, where the former closed his very useful life.   Mr. Corey—one of the best of Christian gentlemen—is living there still, at the age of about 75.

Many thousands of Sunday-Schools owe their origin to the effective labors of Mr. Corey and to his astonishing executive ability.   For thirty years, he acted as agent for the Sunday-School Union, in the West.   It is particularly interesting to me to recall the fact that he was cordially with us in our defence of Mr. Lovejoy's rights in 1837.   II. T.

"with unwavering firmness against a bitter and unscrupulous opposition," had presented petitions against slavery in the House of Representatives. The excitement was so great, and the Southern members so much exasperated by Mr. Adams's pertinacity—for, at times, he presented these petitions, one by one, to the extent of one hundred to two hundred a-day—that he had to meet "a perfect tempest of vituperation and abuse." For report of proceedings which give a fair indication of the state of feeling, see chapter xxiv.,

Then Texas had been wrested from Mexico by the aid of slaveholders, in order to bring that wide region into the Union, for the purpose of increasing slave territory, and maintaining the preponderance of Southern influence in Congress.

Opposition to the project created the bitterest feelings among free-soil men at the North.

Although it may seem strange now, there was good reason then why Lovejoy should maintain his position at Alton. Patriotic defenders of free speech were decided in their advice to him to stand firmly to the last, irrespective of the consequences. It is necessary to bear in mind this actual condition of things in the United States, in order to comprehend the fact that Mr. Lovejoy was firm, but not obstinate.

He always manifested a disposition to weigh carefully and candidly the counsel of friends.

Lovejoy's paper had nearly doubled its circulation by the removal to Alton, which fact he knew was attributable to his decided course. It was not strange, therefore, that, by request, he consented to issue the following call to all friends of the slave in Illinois, asking them to canvas their neighborhood in order to secure signatures to petitions for the abolition of slavery in the District of Columbia.

"DISTRICT OF COLUMBIA PETITIONS.

"We have received from the secretary of the American Anti-Slavery Society, a communication requesting that we would endeavor to forward to them, as soon as possible, the names of two individuals in every county of the State, who will be disposed to receive and circulate petitions to Congress for the abolition of slavery in the District of Columbia.

"We shall send on such names as we are able to designate by our own knowledge, immediately; but as there are many counties in the State where we have no acquaintance, we take this method of asking the attention of all the friends of humanity to the subject.   We suggest the following:

"1. Let all such individuals as are willing to undertake this work, forward their names to us, immediately, free of postage, stating particularly their county, and post-office address.

"2. Where the individual so writing is unknown to us, let him name some respectable individual in this place to whom we can refer, or if he can not do this, in some other way forward to us satisfactory credentials.   This is absolutely necessary to guard against imposition.

"3. Let every individual who volunteers to engage in this work of circulating petitions, do it with the full understanding that it will cost him some time, some trouble, and the good-will of every advocate of slavery. And if he is not willing to undertake the business at this expense, he had better not attempt it at all. And, moreover, let each one sending his name, send also the names of such other individuals, in his own or adjoining counties, as he may think willing and qualified to circulate these petitions with zeal and success.

"We need not add a word touching the vast importance of this subject. With slavery in the several States we have nothing to do, except in the way of argument and persuasion; but let every free man in this republic remember that so long as slavery exists in the District of Columbia, he is himself a slaveholder, and a licenser of the horrid traffic in slaves, carried on under the very shadow of the capitol's walls. We have a right to interfere there, and that right brings with it a solemn duty, which we may not innocently neglect."—*Observer, June 29, 1837.*

The opposition which this call provoked among Southern men who had settled at Alton was great, but it was excessively increased the following week when he presented to his readers reasons for forming, without further delay, an Illinois State Anti-Slavery Society.

To the concurrent advice of many ministerial friends, the publication of this—the most obnoxious of all his editorials—is due. It appeared on July 6, 1837, just after a great Temperance and Sunday-School celebration at Alton, in which leading citizens of various shades of opinion had harmoniously participated:

"ILLINOIS STATE ANTI-SLAVERY SOCIETY.

(The most obnoxious of Mr. Lovejoy's articles.)

"Is it not time that such a society should be formed? There are many, very many, friends of the cause in this State, and their number is daily increasing. Ought not measures to be taken to embody their influence so as to make it tell with the greatest possible effect upon the holy cause of emancipation?

"We would do nothing rashly, but it does seem to us that the time to form such a society has fully come. There are a number of local societies already existing in the State, and it would be every way better that their influence should be concentrated. If it be decided that such a society ought to be formed, when and where shall the convention meet to form it? Shall it be at this place, or at Jacksonville, or Springfield, or elsewhere?

"We take the liberty to throw out these questions for the consideration of our friends, and we suggest the propriety of their giving to them a speedy and candid consideration. Let as many as are in favor of the measure here proposed, send us their names, for the purpose of having them attached to the call of the proposed convention, and let each one indicate the time and place of his preference for the meeting of the convention, with the express understanding that that place shall be selected which has the most votes in its favor.

"We shall hope to have a response from the friends of the slave without delay. Every day do we feel more and more the necessity of action, decided and effective action, on this subject. With many, we are already a 'fanatic' and an 'incendiary,' as it regards this matter, and we feel that we must become more and more vile in their eyes.

"We have never felt enough, nor prayed enough, nor done enough, in behalf of the perishing slave.

"This day (the 4th) reproaches our sloth and inactivity. It is the day of our nation's birth. Even as we write, crowds are hurrying past our window, in eager anticipation, to the appointed bower, to listen to the declaration that 'all men are born free and equal'; to hear the eloquent orator denounce, in strains of manly indignation, the attempt of England to lay a yoke upon the shoulders of our fathers, which neither they nor their children could bear. Alas! what bitter mockery is this. We assemble to thank God for our own freedom, and to eat and drink with joy and gladness of heart, while our feet are upon the necks of nearly three millions of our fellow-men! Not all our shouts of self-congratulation can drown their groans—even that very flag of freedom that waves over our heads is formed from materials cultivated by slaves, on a soil moistened by their blood, drawn from them by the whip of a republican task-master!

"Brethren and friends, this must not be—it can not be—for God will not indure it much longer. Come, then, to the rescue. The voice of three millions of slaves calls upon you to come and 'unloose the heavy burdens, and let the oppressed go free!' And on this day, when every freeman's heart is glad, let us remember that—

"'Wearily every bosom pineth,
Wearily, oh! wearily, oh!

Where the chains of slavery twineth,
  Wearily, oh! wearily, oh!
  There the warrior's dart
    Hath no fleetness,
  There the maiden's heart
    Hath no sweetness.
Every flower of life declineth,
  Wearily, oh! wearily, oh!
  Wearily—wearily—wearily—
  Wearily—wearily—wearily, oh!
    Wearily, oh! wearily, oh!'"

CHAPTER XIII.

The "Market-House" meeting, for the "suppression of Abolitionism"—Comments of the St. Louis press.

Two days after Lovejoy's article, recommending the
formation of a State Anti-Slavery Society, for Illinois, an
anonymous handbill was posted about the city, calling on
those who disapproved the course of the *Alton Observer*
to meet at the public market on July 11, 1837. Of course
this drew together a motley crowd, with a few respectable
citizens. The man who called the meeting to order said
that it was "for the suppression of Abolitionism."

The preamble adopted on the occasion,—written by
some one who was neither correct in grammar nor sound
in sense,—referred to the "spirit of an insulted people
brewing like a cloud and darkening our social atmosphere."
It alluded, in highflown language, to the citizens present,
as having met "to oppose, in a manly manner, this modern
misrule,"—met as "freemen, unseduced by mercenary
motives," etc.

Resolutions were passed disapproving Mr. Lovejoy's
course, and falsely claiming that the man who had again
and again announced that he was ready to die rather than
surrender the right of free speech, had pledged himself not
to discuss the subject of slavery!

Dr. B. K. Hart, L. J. Clawson, N. Buckmaster, A.
Olney, and Dr. J. A. Halderman, were appointed a committee to wait on, and confer with, Mr. Lovejoy, "and

ascertain whether he intends to disseminate through the columns of the *Observer* the doctrine of Abolitionism, and report the result of their conference to the public?" One of the resolutions reported as "cordially adopted," was presented by Col. A. Botkin. It referred to Lovejoy as "persisting to publish an Abolition paper, to the injury of the community," and whilst deprecating the remedy of a mob, he very significantly called on Mr. Lovejoy to "discontinue *his incendiary publications.*" An attempt was made to add the name of the late Benjamin Ives Gilman to the committee, but he declined the honor, and they proceeded in their business without him.

The committee did not seem to relish the idea of a conference with Lovejoy, and neglected to call upon him. After nine days had passed, Mr. Lovejoy published an article calculated to enlighten the minds of these gentlemen. It was entitled, "What are the Doctrines of Anti-Slavery Men?"

Four days subsequent to this, the Market-House Committee succeeded in getting their letter to Lovejoy ready. Without delay Mr. Lovejoy replied, with great kindness and suavity, stating that he could not recognize their right to question him on the liberty of free speech, and he referred them to his article just mentioned, which follows:

WHAT ARE THE DOCTRINES OF ANTI-SLAVERY MEN?

"A young man had become exceedingly angry with an ancient philosopher, and had raised his cane to strike him. 'Strike,' said the philosopher, 'strike, but hear me.' He listened, and was convinced. There is not, probably, an individual, who reads this, that can not recollect some instance in his life, in which his strong opposition to certain measures and principles, he now sees, was entirely owing to groundless and unreasonable prejudices; and he is a fortunate man who can recollect but one such instance. In respect to the subject now to be discussed, the writer frankly confesses no one of his readers can possibly be more prejudiced, or more hostile to anti-slavery measures or men, than he once was. And his, too, were honest, though, alas! how mistaken, prejudices. They arose partly from the fact that the ' new measures' came directly in contact with his former habits of thought and action, and partly, and chiefly, from the strange and astonishingly perverted representations given of leading men and their principles, in this new movement. We recollect no instance of parallel misrepresentation, except the charge brought against Christ of casting out devils by Beelzebub, the prince of devils. These misrepresentations were started by a few, and honestly believed by the many. They still prevail to a very great extent. Very probably some of our readers may be under their influence more or less. We ask them to be candid with themselves, and if they find this to be the case, to make an effort to throw them off, and come to the perusal of what follows, ready to embrace the truth wherever it is found. For truth is eternal, unchanging, though circumstances may, and do, operate to give a different color to it, in our view, at different times. And truth will prevail, and those who do not yield to it must be destroyed by it. What, then, are the doctrines of anti-slavery men?

"FIRST PRINCIPLES.

"1. Abolitionists hold that 'all men are born free and equal, endowed by their Creator with certain inalienable rights, among which are life, LIBERTY, and the pursuit of happiness.' They do not believe that these rights are abrogated, or at all modified, by the color of the skin, but that they extend alike to every individual of the human family.

"2. As the above-mentioned rights are in their nature inalienable, it is not possible that one man can convert another into a piece of property, thus at once annihilating all his personal rights, without the most flagrant injustice and usurpation.   But American slavery does this,—it declares a slave to be a ' THING,' a 'CHATTEL,' an article of personal 'PROPERTY,' a piece of 'MERCHANDISE,' and now actually holds TWO AND A-HALF MILLIONS of our fellow-men in this precise condition.

"3. Abolitionists, therefore, hold American slavery to be a wrong, a legalized system of inconceivable injustice, and a SIN.   That it is a sin against God, whose prerogative as the rightful owner of all human beings is usurped, and against the slave himself, who is deprived of the power to dispose of his services, as conscience may dictate or his Maker require.   And as whatever is morally wrong can never be politically right, and as the bible teaches, and as Abolitionists believe, that 'righteousness exalteth a nation, while sin is a reproach to any people,' they also hold that slavery is a political evil of unspeakable magnitude, and one which, if not removed, will speedily work the downfall of our free institutions, both civil and religious.

"4. As the Bible inculcates upon man but one duty in respect to sin, and that is immediate repentance; Abolitionists believe that all who hold slaves, or who approve the practice in others, should *immediately* cease to do so.

"5. Lastly, Abolitionists believe that as all men are *born* free, so all who are now held as slaves in this country were BORN FREE, and that they are slaves now is the sin, not of those who introduced the race into this country, but of those, and those alone, who now hold them, and have held them in slavery from their birth. Let it be admitted, for argument's sake, that A or B, has justly forfeited his title to freedom, and that he is now the rightful slave of C, bought with his money, how does this give C a claim to the posterity of A, down to the latest generation? And does not the guilt of enslaving the successive generations of A's posterity belong to their respective masters, whoever they be? Nowhere are the true principles of freedom and personal rights better understood than at the South, though their practice corresponds so wretchedly with their theory. Abolitionists adopt, as their own, the following sentiments, expressed by Mr. Calhoun, in a speech on the tariff question, delivered in the Senate of the United States, in 1833: 'He who *earns* the money,—*who digs it out of the earth* with the sweat of his brow, has a *just title* to it against the universe. *No* one has a right to touch it, *without his consent*, except his government, and *it only* to the extent of its legitimate wants; to take more is *robbery*' Now, this is precisely what slave-holders do, and Abolitionists do but echo back their own language when they pronounce it 'robbery.'"

EMANCIPATION—WHAT IS MEANT BY IT?

"Simply, that the slaves shall cease to be held as *property*, and shall henceforth be held and treated as human beings. Simply, that we should take our feet from off their necks. Perhaps we can not express ourselves better than to quote the language of another Southerner. In reply to the question, what is meant by emancipation, the answer is:

'1. It is to reject with indignation the wild and guilty phantasy, that man can hold *property* in man.

'2. To pay the laborer his hire, for he is worthy of it.

'3. No longer to deny him the right of marriage, but to 'let every man have his own wife,' as saith the apostle.

'4. To let parents have their own children, for they are the gift of the Lord *to them*, and no one else has any right to them.

'5. No longer to withhold the advantages of education, and the privilege of reading the bible.

'6. To put the slave under the protection of law, instead of throwing him beyond its salutary influence.'

"Now, who is there that is opposed to slavery at all, and believes it to be wrong and a sin, but will agree to all this?

"HOW AND BY WHOM IS EMANCIPATION TO BE EFFECTED?

"To this question the answer is, by the *masters themselves*, and by no others. No others can effect it, nor is it desirable that they should, even if they could. Emancipation, to be of any value to the slave, must be the free, voluntary act of the master, performed from a conviction of its propriety. This avowal may sound very strange to those who have been in the habit of taking the principles of the Abolitionists from the misrepresentations of their opponents. Yet this is, and always has been, the cardinal principle of Abolitionists. If it be asked, then, why they intermeddle in a matter where they can confessedly do nothing themselves, in achieving the desired result? their reply is, that this is the very reason why they do and ought to intermeddle. It is because they can not emancipate the slaves, that they call upon those who can to do it. Could they themselves do it, there would be no need of discussion; instead of discussing they would act, and with their present views, the work would soon be accomplished.

"Who are they that hold temperance meetings, form temperance societies, sustain and edit, and circulate temperance 'Intelligencers' and 'Heralds'? Are they the men who own distilleries, or who sell or drink ardent spirits by the wholesale or retail? Directly the reverse. They are men who have been convinced of the evil and the sin of such practices, and having quit them themselves, are now endeavoring to persuade their neighbors to do the same thing. For what purpose are the very efficient Executive Committee of the Illinois State Temperance Society now publishing their *Herald*, and endeavoring to send it into every family of the State? Avowedly for the purpose of shutting up every distillery and dram-shop in the State. The object is a noble one, and we bid them God-speed; but how do they purpose to accomplish it? By doing violence, or exciting an angry community to do violence, to the persons or property of their fellow-citizens?

By no manner of means. They would not, if they could, shut up a single grog-shop belonging to their neighbors—and in this thing, all the inhabitants of the State, yea, of the world, are their neighbors—but they wish, and are determined, if light, and love, and argument, and fact, and demonstration can effect it, to persuade all to abandon a business so detrimental to all concerned in it, and to the community at large. Now, this is precisely the ground occupied by Abolitionists in relation to slavery. And let it be remembered, that the objection of interfering in the business of others applies with equal force to the one as to the other. Should the friends of temperance succeed, they will deprive many a man of what is now a very profitable business, and so will the Abolitionists. But in both cases the result will be achieved with the hearty and glad acquiescence of those more immediately concerned, and a great common good will be effected, infinitely over-balancing the partial evil, if evil it may be called, to deprive a man of the profits arising from rum-selling or slave-trading.

"But, in the second place, as to the *particular mode* of effecting emancipation. This, too, belongs to the master to decide. When we tell a distiller, or a vender of ardent spirits, that duty requires him to forsake his present business, we go no further. It belongs not to the preacher of temperance to dictate to them what particular use they shall make of those materials now so improperly employed. He may do any thing, convert his buildings and appurtenances to any use, so that it be a lawful one. Yet advice might, perhaps, be kindly given and profitably listened to. We can tell the slave-holder what he may do with his slaves after emancipation, so as to do them just-ice, and at the same time, lose nothing himself. Employ them as free laborers, pay them their stipulated wages, and the results of the West-India emancipation have af-forded to us the means of assuring him that he will derive more clear profit from their labor as freemen than as slaves. Did the Abolitionists propose to remove the slave population from the country, the free inhabitants of the South might justly complain; for that would soon render their country a barren and uncultivated waste. But they aim at no such thing; nor yet would they encourage or allow the emancipated slaves to roam about the country as idle vagabonds; they would say to them, as to others, 'They that will not work, neither shall they eat,' and let the regulation be enforced with all proper sanctions. Only when they work, let them be paid for it.

"No charge has been more perseveringly made, or con-tributed more to render the cause of emancipation odious, than that 'its friends were also advocates of the amalgama-tion of the two races.' Now, in answer to this, we reply:

"1. The charge comes with an exceedingly bad grace from those who are loudest in making it; since they, that is many of them (we speak within bounds when we say more than half of them), do not only advocate, but actual-ly practise amalgamation. The evidence of this is written in the bleached countenances of the slaves throughout all the slave-holding region. The law of slave descent is, that the children follow the condition of the mother; and the consequence is, that thousands hold as slaves their own sons and daughters, and brothers and sisters, and nephews and nieces. We know several cases of this sort. The Vice-President of the United States has been, if he is not now, the father of slaves. And thousands have voted to elevate him to his present condition, who would crucify an Abolitionist on the bare suspicion of favoring, though only in theory, such an amalgamation. How shall we account for such inconsistency?

"2. But, secondly, the charge is untrue—completely, and absolutely, and in every sense untrue. Abolitionists do not advocate the doctrine of amalgamation, but the reverse. And nothing can be more unjust than thus to charge them, without the least shadow of truth to sustain the charge. On the contrary, one reason why Abolitionists urge the abolition of slavery is, that they fully believe it will put a stop, in a great, and almost entire measure, to that wretched, and shameful, and polluted intercourse between the whites and blacks, now so common, it may be said so universal, in the slave States. As to equality of privileges, immunities, etc., the question of emancipation has nothing to do with these questions at all. Abolitionists are not so silly as to suppose that merely setting the slaves free will at once make learned, virtuous, and influential individuals out of the degraded mass of slaves. They know better, though, at the same time, they believe a process of purification and elevation would commence, which would gradually be productive of the most beneficial consequences. The question of civil rights is one entirely distinct from that of personal rights. Let the latter be restored and guaranteed, and the whole object of the Abolitionists, as such, is accomplished. Political rights are alienable, personal rights are not. Personal rights are often as secure under the government of a despot—Frederick the Great, of Prussia, for instance,—as they possibly can be any where; while at the same time the subject has no political rights, give him these and you allow him to pursue his own happiness in his own way, provided he seeks it not at the expense of others. If in this pursuit he becomes the most virtuous, the most learned, the most eloquent, the most influential man in the United States, we see not how it is to be helped, nor who has a right to obstruct his course.

"The above exposition of anti-slavery principles has been made at the request of a number of our respectable citizens. In preparing it, we have felt deeply our responsibility, and have trembled lest through any inadvertence of language we should make ourselves liable to be misunderstood, and thus repel the minds of those whom we wish to gain. In the correctness of these principles we have the most unshaken confidence, and that they finally will be properly understood and most universally adopted by our countrymen, we have no more doubt than we have that Washington lived, and Warren died, to secure the blessings of civil and religious liberty. That they have met with such determined opposition, and brought upon their prominent supporters such extreme manifestations of popular hatred, is partly, and chiefly, owing to the fact that they have been strangely misapprehended, and partly that, in their practical application in this country, they strike, or are supposed to strike, at self-interests of great magnitude.

"Until the sentiments and principles set forth above shall prevail over the earth, the world can never be delivered from the bondage under which it has so long groaned. They are the sentiments which, though oftentimes dimly and feebly apprehended, have actuated the minds of the great and good of every age, who have mourned over the degredation of human nature, and have sought to elevate it, by ascertaining and securing those rights of man with which his Maker has endowed him. They are the principles which actuated a Thrasybulus, an Epaminondas, a Spartacus, and a Brutus, of antiquity; a Doria, a Tell, a Hampden, a Sidney, a Russell, a Hancock, an Adams, a Washington, of later days. They brought our pilgrim fathers from the homes and firesides of old England to this country, then an unknown land, and a waste, howling wilderness. They sustained them to endure toils, and hardships, and privations, until they made the 'wilderness to rejoice and blossom as the rose.' And now shall their children forsake these principles, and attempt to roll back the wheels of that reformation on whose banner is inscribed the LIBERTY AND EQUALITY OF THE HUMAN RACE, and which dispenses in its train, alike to all, the blessings of peace, of harmony, and the unmolested rights of conscience? No, they will not, they dare not.

"We do not mean to be understood than in the cases referred to above, the manifestations of these principles were always proper. Enough, however, appeared to show that the minds of these patriots and sages were communing with their Maker, and were receiving from Him,— though owing to the darkness of their minds, imperfectly understood and often misapprehended,—revelations of the rights, duties, and privileges which He designed for the race.

> "Did the forms
> Of servile custom cramp their gen'rous powers?
> Would sordid policies, the barb'rous growth
> Of ignorance and rapine, bow them down
> To tame pursuits, to indolence and fear?
> Lo! they appeal to nature, to the winds
> And rolling waves, the sun's unwearied course,
> The elements and seasons; all declare
> For what the eternal Maker has ordain'd
> The powers of man; they felt within themselves
> His energy divine.

"These principles, then, are eternal and immutable, for they are established by God himself, and whoever would destroy them, must first reach up to heaven and dethrone the Almighty. Sin had wellnigh banished them from the earth, when the Son of God came down to reassert them, and died to sanction them. They are summed up, perfectly, in the language by which the angels announced the object of the Redeemer's mission: 'GLORY TO GOD IN THE HIGHEST. ON EARTH PEACE, GOOD WILL TOWARD MEN.'"

COMMENTS OF THE ST. LOUIS PRESS.

The *Missouri Republican*, of St. Louis, was very generally taken and read at Alton, at that time. The proceedings of the market-house meeting were published in that paper, and commented on in a way to encourage a spirit of lawlessness and outrage, as follows:

"THE ALTON MEETING.

"We give to-day all of the proceedings of the meeting held in Alton, on Thursday last, that our space will permit. We rejoice to see our neighbors taking this subject into hand. The proceedings of the meeting speak for themselves. They are not the intemperate ebullitions of excitement, or the temporary expression of a high-wrought feeling; on the contrary, the proceedings throughout, manifest, to us, the deep and settled purpose of men whose hospitalities have been slighted, and whose friendships have been abused by one who was bound by every moral and political obligation to have acted otherwise. The editor of the *Observer* has merited the full measure of the community's indignation; and if he will not learn from experience, they are very likely to teach him by practice, something of the light in which the honorable and respectable portion of the community view his conduct. He has, by his adhesion to the odious doctrines of Abolitionism, of which faction he now avows himself a member, and by his continued efforts to disseminate these odious doctrines, forfeited all claims to the protection of that or any other community."

THE ST. LOUIS REPUBLICAN'S SECOND ARTICLE IN FAVOR OF "DOING SOMETHING."

The *Republican's* hints had not led to the ejection of Lovejoy from Alton, and on August 17, 1837,—four days before the destruction of his second press,—they published plainer directions, declaring that "something must be done," and that speedily, as follows:

"ANTI-SLAVERY SOCIETIES IN ILLINOIS.

"We perceive that an Anti-Slavery Society has been formed at Upper-Alton, and many others, doubtless, will shortly spring up in different parts of the State. We had hoped that our neighbors would have ejected from amongst them that minister of mischief, the *Observer*, or at least corrected its course.

"Something must be done in this matter, and that speedily! The good people of Illinois must either put a stop to the efforts of these fanatics, or expel them from their community. If this is not done, the travel of emigrants through their State, and the trade of the slaveholding States, and particularly Missouri, must stop. Every one who desires the harmony of the country, and the peace and prosperity of all, should unite to put them down. They can do no positive good, and may do much irreparable harm. We would not desire to see this done at the expense of public order or legal restraint; but there is a moral indignation which the virtuous portion of a community may exert, which is sufficient to crush this faction and forever disgrace its fanatic instigators. It is to this we appeal, and hope that the appeal will not be unhedeed."

CHAPTER XIV.

Lovejoy mobbed—Destruction of the second press—Lovejoy of-
fers to resign as editor—His offer not accepted—A third
press ordered—Its destruction—Lovejoy again mobbed—A
thrilling narrative—A fourth press ordered.

The spirit of insubordination was, at this time, increasing throughout the land, as the result of a general conflict
of opinion on the subject of slavery.

The market-house meeting at Alton, and the persist-
ency with which St. Louis newspapers declared that "something must be done," naturally led to a mob at Alton, on
August 21, 1837. The rabble first attempted to assault
Mr. Lovejoy at nine o'clock in the evening, as he was returning from the apothecary's with some medicine for his
sick wife. His account of the attempt reads as follows:
"We reside more than half a mile from town. And just
as I was leaving the principal street I met the mob. They
did not at first recognize me, and I parted their columns
for some distance, and had just reached the rear, when
some of them began to suspect who it was. They immediately wheeled their column and came after me; I did
not hurry at all, believing it was not for such a man as I
am to flee. They seemed a little loath to come on me,
and I could hear their leaders swearing at them, and telling them to 'push on,' etc. By this time, they began to
throw clods of dirt at me, and several hit, without hurting
me. And now a fellow pushed up to my side, armed with

a club, to ascertain certainly who it was.   He then yelled
out, 'It's the d—d Abolitionist, give him hell;' whereat
there was another rush upon me.   But when they got close
up, they seemed again to fall back.   At length, a number
of them, linked arm in arm, pushed by me and wheeled in
the road before me, thus stopping me completely.   I then
spoke to them, asking them why they stopped me.   By
this time the cry was all around me, 'd—n him,' 'rail him,'
'rail him,' 'tar and feather him,' 'tar and feather him.'   I
had no doubt that such was to be my fate,   I then said to
them, I have one request to make of you, and then you
may do with me what you please.   I then asked them to
send one of their number to take the medicine to my wife,
which I begged they would do without alarming her.
This they promised, and sent one of their number to do
it, who did it according to the promise.   I then said to
them, 'you had better let me go; you have no right to de-
tain me; I have never injured you.'   They began to curse
and to swear, when I added, 'I am in your hands, and you
must do with me whatever God permits you to do.'"

The sublime calmness of the man whose soul is stayed
on God proved in this case—as it frequently has before—
the prelude to deliverance.   God disappointed the "devices of the crafty, so that their hands could not perform
their enterprise."   They consulted a few moments, and
then bade Lovejoy go home.

During the same night, at a little later hour, a mob entered the *Observer* office, destroyed the press, type, and
material, and wounded one of the men, by casting a stone
through the window.   Immediately after this, assurances

of aid—not a few from distant States—came freely to Mr. Lovejoy. His ministerial brethren expressed the earnest wish, and confident expectation, that his paper should go on, and the friends of free-speech at once held a meeting for that object at Alton.

Money was offered for another press, and so quickly was the order executed, that the new material arrived at Alton on September 21, 1837, at a time when Mr. Lovejoy was absent at Presbytery. This was the third press, and some of the friends in Alton began to doubt the wisdom of Lovejoy's continuance in the position of editor. The abatement of zeal and partial desertion among his friends were largely caused by the circulation of a pamphlet by the Rev. Mr. Smylie,* which was said to be "full of gross perversions, yet gilded over with a smirking cant of sincerity." This tract, with a specious sophistry well calculated to deceive, endeavored to prove that the bible sanctions the system of American slavery. Shakespeare evidently had such reverend seniors in mind when he made Bassanio say:

> "In religion,
> What damned error, but some sober brow,
> Will bless it and approve it with a text."

Rev. Joel Parker, of New Orleans, was at Alton about this time, and he also exerted an influence which was adverse to Mr. Lovejoy.

The question, however, was not one of abolition doctrine, but whether the free use of the press—whether civil liberty, for which so much blood had been shed, and so many pri-

* Of Mississippi.

vations had been encountered in the United States, was to
be surrendered at the dictation of slave-holders. That was
the question, and it is a fact that many of those—myself
included—who took the most active part in sustaining Mr.
Lovejoy were not then Abolitionists.

As soon as Lovejoy ascertained that there was a difference of sentiment among his friends, he decided to make
an unconditional surrender of the editorship; but, finally,
on the judicious advice of one in particular, he concluded to
leave the question to be decided by all of his friends, and to
cheerfully yield his post to a successor, if that was desired.
This decision was communicated in the following letter:

OFFER TO RESIGN THE EDITORIAL CHAIR.

"TO THE FRIENDS OF THE REDEEMER IN ALTON.

"ALTON, September 11th, 1837.

"DEAR BRETHREN:

"It is at all times important that the friends of truth should
be united. It is especially so, at the present time, when
iniquity is coming in like a flood. I should be false to my
covenant vows, and false to every feeling of my heart, were
I to refuse making any personal sacrifice to effect so desirable an object. Having learned that there is a division of
sentiments among the brethren, as it regards the propriety
of my continuing longer to fill the office of editor of the
Alton Observer, I do not hesitate a moment to submit
the question to your decision. Most cheerfully will I resign my post if, in your collective wisdom, you think the
cause we all profess to love will thereby be promoted. And
in coming to a decision on this question, I beseech you as
a favor—may I not enjoin it as a duty?—that you act with-

out any regard to my personal feelings. I should be false
to the Master I serve, and of whose gospel I am a minister,
should I allow my own interests (real or supposed) to be
placed in competition with His. Indeed, I have no interest, no wish, at least, I think I have none; I know I ought
to have none other than such as are subordinate to his will.
Be it yours, brethren, to decide what is best for the cause
of truth, most for the glory of God and the salvation of
souls, and rest assured—whatever my own private judgment may be—of my cordial acquiescence in your decision.

"I had, at first, intended to make an *unconditional* surrender of the editorship into your hands. But as such a
course might be liable to misconstructions, I have, by the
advice of a beloved brother, determined to leave the whole
matter with you. I am ready to go forward if you say so,
and equally ready to yield to a successor, if such be your
opinion. Yet let me say, promptly, that in looking back
over my past labors as editor of the *Observer*, while I see
many imperfections and many errors and mistakes, I have,
nevertheless, done the best I could. This I say in the fear
of God; so that if I am to continue the editor, you must
not, on the whole, expect a much better paper than you
have had.

"Should you decide that I ought to give place to a successor, I shall expect the two following conditions to be
fulfilled:

"1. That you will assume in its behalf all my obligations
contracted in consequence of my connection with the *Observer*. Some of them were contracted immediately on
behalf of the *Observer*, and some in supporting my family
while its editor.

"2. As I have now spent four, among the best years of my life, in struggling to establish the *Observer*, and place it on its present footing, I shall expect you will furnish me with a sum sufficient to enable me to remove myself and family to another field of labor. More I do not ask, and I trust this will not be thought unreasonable. I would not ask even this had I the means myself, but I have not.

"3. On these conditions I surrender into your hands the *Observer's* subscription list, now amounting to more than two thousand one hundred names, and constantly increasing, together with all the dues coming to the establishment. A list both of the debts and credits accompanies this communication. May the spirit of wisdom, dear brethren, guide you to a wise and *unanimous* decision—to a decision which God will approve and ratify, and which shall redound to the glory of His name.

"Yours affectionately,

"ELIJAH P. LOVEJOY."

A meeting of the friends was accordingly held which, after adjournment and long consideration of the subject, gave it as their opinion that the *Observer* should be re-established, and Elijah P. Lovejoy ought to continue its editor.

The third press, as I have stated, arrived at Alton about sunset on September 21st, 1837, during the absence of Mr. Lovejoy. Many of his friends gathered around it as it was conveyed to the warehouse of Gerry & Weller. No violence was offered, but cries of "There goes the Abolition press, stop it," were heard. The mayor, John M. Krum,

seemed desirous of protecting it, and asked that it be left
in his hands. The provision he made, however, was entirely inadequate. He had a constable posted at the door of
Gerry's warehouse, until a certain hour in the night. As
soon as this official left, ten or twelve "respectable" ruffians,
disguised with handkerchiefs over their faces, broke into
the store, rolled out the press to the river-bank, broke all
up and cast it into the Mississippi. The mayor, however,
arrived before all was destroyed, and told them to disperse.
They replied to the effect that they were *busy*, and as soon
as through with their little job they would go home, and
they recommended him to do the same without delay. This
he did, remarking, it is said, that he never had witnessed a
more quiet and gentlemanly mob. There were a few gentlemen from the South, at that time, living in Alton, who
gloried in Southern institutions and Southern domination,
and it was not difficult for such men to find followers at the
saloons in the City, or to procure aid from the neighboring
City of St. Louis. It was said, that in the month of August
preceding, a party of armed men had come from St. Louis
and stationed themselves behind a wall for the purpose of
firing on any one who should dare to defend Lovejoy's
office.

LOVEJOY AGAIN MOBBED.—A FOURTH PRESS ORDERED.

Whilst Lovejoy was sufficiently resolute to go to the
stake with calmness and in peace of mind, because his conscience was at peace with God, he was still exceedingly
sensitive as to the opinions of friends. As it was with
Luther, "Thoughts many and deep, words few," so was it
with him. The poem "Athanasius Contra Mundum" presents a true picture of Lovejoy:

"They call me haughty, of opinion proud,
      Untaught to bend a stubborn will;
Ah! little dreams the shallow-hearted crowd
      What thoughts this bosom fill,
What loneliness this outer strength doth hide,
      What longing lies beneath this calm,
For human sympathy so long untried,
      Our Earth's divinest balm.

But more than sympathy the truth I prize;
      Above my friendships hold I God,
And stricken be these feet ere they despise
      The path their Maker trod.
So let my banner be again unfurled,
      Again its cheerless motto seen,
'*The world against me, I against the world:*'
      Judge Thou, dear Christ, between."
      [Translated by the REV. W. R. HUNTINGTON.]

We have reason to believe that at times, like Job, he prayed for death, yet in perfect submission to the divine will.

It is by no means pleasant for me to record particulars of riots and persecutions, and therefore I shall give but a very brief account of the mob which occurred at St. Charles, Missouri, about ten days after the destruction of his third press, by which Mr. Lovejoy nearly lost his life.

His mother-in-law lived in that city, and he and his sick wife, with their infant, were staying with her. Mr. Lovejoy had preached twice on that quiet Sabbath, and about nine at night, when he and his friend, Rev. Mr. Campbell, were conversing, they heard an ominous knock at the door and a call for Mr. Lovejoy. He answered "I am here."

They immediately rushed up the portico, and two of them, coming into the room (wrote Mr. Lovejoy), "laid hold of me. These two individuals, the name of one was Littler, formerly from Virginia, the other called himself a Mississippian, but his name I have not learned, though it is known in St. Charles. I asked them what they wanted of me. 'We want you down stairs, d——n you,' was the reply. They accordingly commenced attempting to pull me out of the house. And not succeeding immediately, one of them, Littler, began to beat me with his fists. By this time, Mrs. Lovejoy had come into the room. In doing so, she had to make her way through the mob on the portico, who attempted to hinder her from coming by rudely pushing her back, and one 'chivalrous' Southerner actually drew his dirk upon her. Her only reply was to strike him in the face with her hand, and then, rushing past him, she flew to where I was, and, throwing her arms around me, boldly faced the mobites, with a fortitude and self-devotion which none but a woman and a wife ever displayed. While they were attempting with oaths and curses to drag me from the room, she was smiting them in the face with her hands, or clinging to me to aid in resisting their efforts, and telling them that they must first take her before they should have her husband. Her energetic measures, seconded by those of her mother and sister, induced the assailants to let me go and leave the room.

As soon as they were gone, Mrs. Lovejoy's powers of endurance failed her, and she fainted. I carried her into another room and laid her on the bed. So soon as she recovered from her fainting she relapsed into hysterical fits,

moaning and shrieking and calling upon my name alter-
nately. Her situation at this time was truly alarming and
distressing. To add to the perplexities of the moment, I
had our sick child in my arms, taken up from the floor,
where it had been left by its grandmother, in the hurry and
alarm of the first onset of the mob. The poor little sufferer, as if conscious of danger from the cries of its mother,
clung to me in silence. In this condition, and while I was
endeavoring to calm Mrs. Lovejoy's dreadfully excited
mind, the mob returned to the charge, breaking into the
room, and, rushing up to the bedside, again attempting to
force me from the house. The brutal wretches were total-
ly indifferent to her heart-rending cries and shrieks—she
was too far exhausted to move; and I suppose they would
have succeeded in forcing me out, had not my friend,
William M. Campbell, at this juncture come in, and with
undaunted boldness, assisted me in freeing myself from
their clutches. Mr. Campbell is a Southerner and a slave-
holder; but he is a *man*, and he will please accept my grateful thanks for his aid so promptly and so opportunely ren-
dered; others aided in forcing the mob from the room, so
that the house was now clear a second time.

They did not, however, leave the yard of the house,
which was full of drunken wretches, uttering the most awful and soul-chilling oaths and imprecations, and swearing
they would have me at all hazards. I could hear the epithets, 'The infernal scoundrel, the d——d amalgamating
Abolitionist, we'll have his heart out yet,' etc., etc. They
were armed with pistols and dirks, and one pistol was discharged, whether at any person or not, I did not know.
The fellow from Mississippi seemed the most bent on my

destruction. He did not appear at all drunken, but both in words and actions manifested the most fiendish malignity of feeling and purpose."

The drunken rabble filled the door-yard; three times they returned to the attack, after which Lovejoy's friends insisted on his leaving the place that night. It was very dark, but he groped his way to the house of Major Sibley, his friend, a mile distant, where he was furnished with a horse, and by daylight he reached the dwelling of the excellent Elder Watson, and from thence proceeded to Alton, commending his wife and child to the tender mercy of his God. Thus it will be seen that with the principles which he felt it his duty to avow he was not safe anywhere. He stood as the bold representative of civil and religious liberty and learned "by the things which he suffered" that they who will "live godly in Christ Jesus shall suffer persecution."

From this time to his martyrdom was but little more than a month. In that space of time, Lovejoy resigned himself to the advice of friends. He neither sought nor shunned position. Another press, the fourth and last, had been ordered, through the aid of the defenders of free-speech in Ohio, as was believed.

Where the press was to be used was not decided. The friends of the Anti-Slavery cause were to meet at Upper-Alton, in convention, on Oct. 26th, 1837, to form a State Anti-Slavery Society. To God, and to his ministerial brethren who were to attend that gathering, he committed his way, ready to give place to another, to remove to Quincy, Ill., to which place he had been invited,—or to pursue any other course that Providence might indicate.

CHAPTER XV.

An anti-slavery convention called—Proceedings of the Convention—Colonization meetings—President Edward Beecher,
of Illinois College, defends Mr. Lovejoy—His address interrupted—A mob prevented by armed citizens.

On the third week of October, 1837, Mr. Lovejoy attended the annual meeting of synod, at Springfield, Illinois,
where he had an opportunity to counsel with his brethren
regarding his future course.

He returned to Alton greatly refreshed by their en-
couragement and approbation. About two hundred and
fifty persons, some of them aged clergymen, whose views
he respected, had signed the call for the Anti-Slavery
Convention, and as his fourth press would not arrive until
after the time of that meeting, he looked to his friends to
decide from what point in the State the future numbers of
the *Alton Observer* should issue. The convention which
had been called to establish a State Anti-Slavery Society,
met on October 26, 1837, in the Presbyterian Church, in
Upper-Alton.

The call for members was unfortunately so wide, that
the instigators and abettors of the mobs, and even the actors in them, found no difficulty in gaining entrance. They
had formed the cunning device of presenting themselves
in such force as to rule the assembly. The Rev. Gideon
Blackburn, then very old, but an excellent man, was called
by general consent to the chair. There was a majority of

the friends of the call then in the house, but much delay
was occasioned, and an entire afternoon was spent in heated
discussion.

The next morning, the chairman decided that the previous day's meeting had been disorderly, and that the test of
membership must be signature to the call.   Many signed
who desired to break up the convention, and the Attorney-
General, U. F. Linder, succeeded in having himself put on
the business committee, with two good men as associates,—
Rev. Edward Beecher and Rev. Mr. Turner.   This, of
course, led to two reports, and the minority report was
carried by Linder's and Rev. John Hogan's followers, who
then adjourned the convention *sine die*.

But this farce could not succeed with such earnest men.
The real friends of the convention met at the house of
Rev. T. B. Hurlburt, formed a State Society, appointing E.
P. Lovejoy corresponding secretary, and after a full discussion of the subject, decided to recommend Mr. Lovejoy
to continue the publication of his paper at Alton.   Many,
however, were opposed to settling the question in this
manner, unless the civil authorities and people of Alton
would awaken to the importance of sustaining law against
mob-rule.   It was thought prudent that whenever the press
arrived it should be stored in the warehouse of Godfrey
& Gilman, though nothing had been said to them on the
subject.   There, it was believed, it would be safe from the
vengeance of mobs, because of the high standing of the
firm, and because it was not decided yet whether Mr.
Lovejoy might not take it to Quincy, Ill.

Just before, and immediately after the date of the con-

vention, some good men who called themselves coloniza-
tionists, and a number of others whose motives were ques-
tioned, became possessed with a sudden glow in favor
of colonization.   Two meetings were held about this time
in Upper and in Lower-Alton, the object of which seemed
to be to forestall the Abolitionists.

They were addressed by Hon. Cyrus Edwards, Rev. J.
M. Peck, and Rev. Joel Parker, the latter of New Orleans.
It was reported that Dr. Parker even went so far as to say
that it is "an un-Christian thing to speak on any subject
calculated greatly to disturb and agitate a people," thus
making in effect the same objection to Lovejoy that the
Thessalonians made to Paul, when they called out, "these
that have turned the world upside down, have come hither
also."

On the 30th of October, a day or two after the colonization meeting, the friends of free-speech were addressed by
Rev. Edward Beecher, then President of Illinois College,
at the Presbyterian church, in Lower-Alton.   He expressed himself strongly in favor of defending Mr. Lovejoy to the last, and his views exerted a powerful influence
upon his hearers.   Mr. Beecher's discourse was interrupted
for a short time in consequence of a stone being cast
through one of the church windows, and he probably
would have been mobbed then, but for the fact that the
mayor was in the meeting, and we had made provision to
repel any attack.   The moment the stone was thrown my
brother, who was in the gallery, called our company "To
arms!" and in a few moments the church door was flanked
on either side by a row of armed men, whom it was not

safe for a mob to attack.   Enoch Long and A. W. Corey
were among the citizens in line.   Mr. Beecher went on
with his discourse to the close, and as the people retired,
the mayor called on outsiders to disperse.   The prompt-
ness of this defence was due to the fact that after repeated
consultations between the mayor, Mr. Lovejoy, Mr. Gilman, myself and others, we had organized a company of
about fifty men, a part of whom were afterwards in service
in Godfrey & Gilman's warehouse on the night of the
mob.   We certainly supposed ourselves acting under civil
authority, because the mayor was not only cognizant of all
our doings, but had stated to us that we had a right to
defend the press, and if it was attacked he would order us
to fire on our assailants.

   Subsequently, at the trial of the defenders of the press,
Mayor Krum stated that in those interviews we must have
misunderstood him.   He said that his advice to us was
that of a citizen and a friend, but he did not consider he
was then advising us officially, as mayor,   This finely-
drawn distinction, made subsequently to the events, presented an unforeseen view of our responsibility—albeit, had
we known this kindly, unofficial advice at the time it was
given, I believe it would have made no difference in the
determination to defend our "castle."

CHAPTER XVI.

The last public meeting—The proceedings and the results—
Comments in *The New York American.*

I have now brought the reader to the 2d November,
1837, when a meeting was held in Alton, which was, evidently, as closely connected with the riot of November 7th,
as cause is with effect. The reader has seen that a mob
was prevented at the Presbyterian Church by means of a
bold defence: it is my deliberate conviction that had the
leading citizens of Alton united with us at this meeting, to
sustain the civil rights of Lovejoy, any mob that could have
been raised might have been overcome.

A full report of meeting—so important in its results—
will be found in appendix, page 18 , and I insert here an
exceedingly clear resumé and criticism of it, which appeared
in the *New-York American*, November 29th, 1837.

THE ALTON MURDER—ITS CAUSE.

"Mr. Editor:—The principal circumstances attendant
on the Alton murder are now before the public, but there
are certain other events which transpired in that place previous to the murder, which, though published in the newspapers of the place, are not so generally known as they
should be.

"To these circumstances I wish to direct the attention
of your readers, and I do not anticipate any difficulty in
establishing between them and the murder the relation of
cause and effect. On Thursday, Nov. 2, a public meeting

of the citizens of Alton was held, 'to take into consideration the present excited state of public feeling in the City,
growing out of the discussion of the Abolition question.'
To this meeting, Mr. W. S. Gilman presented certain resolutions, declaring in substance the right of every citizen to
speak, write, or print his opinions on any subject, being responsible for the abuse of that right to the law administered
by its regular tribunals.   That the maintenance of these
principles should be independent of all regard to persons or
sentiments.   That we are more especially called on to
maintain them in cases of unpopular persons or sentiments, as in any such cases only can effort be required.

"That for these reasons *alone*, and *irrespective of all moral,
political, or religious sentiments*, protection was due to the
person and property of Mr. Lovejoy, the editor of the *Alton
Observer;* that this protection should be afforded on *the
ground of principle solely*, and altogether *disconnected from
approbation of his sentiments*, his personal character, and
his course as editor of the *Alton Observer*.   The adoption
of these resolutions was opposed by U. F. Linder and
others, and they were finally referred to a committee.   To
give time for this committee to report, the meeting adjourned till next day, having first passed a resolution that
if any violence was attempted they would do all in their
power to maintain the law.

"The committee, which was composed of the Attorney-
General of the State, Mr. Edwards, member of the legislature, and several persons of respectable standing, reported
next day that it was inexpedient to pass the resolutions,
that they 'demanded too much and conceded too little,'

that 'there must be a mutual sacrifice of prejudices,' etc.

"Instead of the resolutions of Mr. Gilman, the committee offered six of their own, declaring:

"1.   That it was *expedient* to abstain from a discussion of principles, in themselves deemed right and of the highest importance.

"2.   That the establishment of a properly conducted religious paper would be desirable and approved by the people of Alton.

"3.   That without desiring to restrain the liberty of the press in general, it was *indispensable* that Mr. Lovejoy *should not be allowed* to conduct a paper, and that he ought to retire from the charge of the *Alton Observer*.

"The 6th resolution declared that they would not be understood to reflect on the personal character or motives of Mr. Lovejoy.

"Against these views, Mr. W. S. Gilman, one of the committee, presented a protest. *He was alone.* The resolutions were then put to the meeting, and *that recommending the establishment of a properly-conducted religious newspaper stricken out*, as was the one repudiating all reflections on the personal character of Mr. Lovejoy.

"Thus amended, they passed.   Then followed the usual cold disapproval of all violence.   The meeting was about to adjourn, when the mayor of the city offered a resolution expressive of the regret felt by the citizens of Alton, 'that persons and editors abroad should interest themselves in discussion of matters of which that City was made the theatre.'   Then the meeting adjourned.

"I think, Mr. Editor, that this plain detail, coming ex-

clusively from the "Official Report of the Meeting" (for I
have no other means of obtaining information), established
beyond the possibility of cavil the relation of cause and
effect, between this public meeting of the citizens of Alton
and the murder, which, but four short days afterward, occurred.   What but murder, what but violence could result
from such proceedings?   What could an ignorant and infuriated mob do when thus encouraged by those to whom
they had been accustomed to look up for opinions?   The
mayor, the attorney-general, and the merchants of Alton,
with one proud exception, declared that Mr. Lovejoy ought
not, and must not, be allowed to establish a press—'it is
essential that he should be prevented from doing so'—this
decision goes forth to the mob, but they ask, 'how can he
be prevented?'   Mr. Mayor and his friends reply, for they
can make no other, '*We can not hinder him.*'   To this, what
will be the certain answer of an excited mob?   '*We can—
we will.*'   Was not this the natural, the necessary, the inevitable consequence?   But the resolutions of these Altonians
deserve a moment's consideration.   Certain resolutions had
been laid before the meeting declaring the inalienable right
of every citizen to freedom of speech and freedom of the
press.   That to print and publish his free thoughts was the
birth-right of every American, and that every man should
be protected in this right.   And how does Mr. Legislator
Edwards and Mr. Attorney-General, of the State of Illinois, dispose of these declarations—'they demand too much
and concede too little'—say they.   Demand too much?
They demand freedom—freedom of thought—of speech—
of the press.   Concede too little?   They concede nothing,

and God forbid that, when freedom of speech and the liberty of the press is in question, anything should be conceded.

"But Mr. Edwards says, 'we should mutually sacrifice our prejudices.' And has it indeed come to this? Is it in our land that the freedom of the press is called a *prejudice?* Shame on the word—and double shame on the American tongue that could thus apply it.

"Perhaps you will think, Mr. Editor, that I dwell too long upon these proceedings, and attach too much importance to them. Sir, I wish to hold these proceedings—these resolutions and expressions of opinion—and the riot and murder, which have been their natural result—up as a warning to the American people.

"Did my power bear any proportion to my zeal, these *promptings to murder*, coming from persons holding respectable stations in society, should be held up to the detestation of every American, worthy of the name, and the resolutions in which Americans have dared to stigmatize the freedom of the press and of opinion as 'a *prejudice*,' to the scorn and contempt of every friend of civil liberty throughout the world! One word to Mayor *Krum* and his resolution. The people of Alton, it seems, do not desire that their doings should 'be canvassed by editors and persons at a distance.'

"This is prudent. I wonder not that they should be unwilling to have their conduct commented on by any press out of the reach of their mob violence.

"But the desire is vain. Their acts will be canvassed and condemned far and near, throughout the length and breadth of this free land. The murderer of Mr. Lovejoy will, to all appearance, go unpunished. His murderers are in the majority.

"Mr. Mayor Krum, in his account, which might almost be called apology for the murder, does not hint at the idea of punishing the murderers. But do the people of Alton imagine that, by proclaiming immunity to violence and murder within the limits of their City, they can make murder less detestable, or prevent 'editors and persons at a distance' from denouncing the murderers and all who, before or after, aid or abet in murder? No, sir! They will be commented on, again and again, till Alton and her pusillanimous magistracy, her murderers, and those who prompt to murder, and allow murder to go unpunished, shall attain an infamous notoriety throughout our country.

"CARAGA."

CHAPTER XVII.

Mr. Lovejoy's defence, delivered at the above-mentioned meeting—His calmness—Announcement of his determination to remain in Alton.

The courageous speech made by Mr. Lovejoy, at the meeting described in the previous chapter, is so noble in its fearlessness, and gives one so just an idea of the man's heroism, that I insert it here. His patient bearing at this trying moment is not unaptly described in the language of Shakspeare, concerning Richard II.:

> "No man cried, God save him;
> No joyful tongue gave him his welcome home;
> But dust was thrown upon his sacred head;
> Which with such gentle sorrow he shook off,—
> His face still combating with tears and smiles,
> The badges of his grief and patience,—
> That had not God, for some strong purpose, steel'd
> The hearts of men, they must per force have melted,
> And barbarism itself have pitied him."

A writer who was present, observed: "His *manner*,—but I cannot attempt to describe it. He was calm and serious, but firm and decided. Not an epithet or unkind allusion escaped his lips, notwithstanding he knew he was in the midst of those who were seeking his blood, and notwithstanding he was well aware of the influence that that meeting, if it should not take the right turn, would have in infuriating the mob to do their work. He and his friends had prayed earnestly that God would overrule the deliberations of that meeting for good. He had been all day communing with God. His countenance, the subdued tones of his voice, and whole appearance indicated a mind in a peculiarly heavenly frame, and ready to acquiesce in the will of God, whatever that might be. I confess to you, sir, that I regarded him at the time, in view of all the circumstances, as presenting a spectacle of moral sublimity, such as I had never before witnessed, and such as the world seldom affords. It reminded me of Paul before Festus, and of Luther at the diet of Worms."

He spoke as follows:

"MR. CHAIRMAN:—

"It is not true, as has been charged upon me, that I hold in contempt the feelings and sentiments of this community, in reference to the question which is now agitating it. I respect and appreciate the feelings and opinions of my fellow-citizens, and it is one of the most painful and unpleasant duties of my life, that I am called upon to act in opposition to them. If you suppose, sir, that I have published sentiments contrary to those generally held in this community, because I delighted in differing from them, or in occasioning a disturbance, you have entirely misapprehended me. But, sir, while I value the good opinion of my fellow-citizens, as highly as any one, I may be permitted to say, that I am governed by higher considerations than either the favor or the fear of man. I am impelled to the course I have taken, because I fear God. As I shall answer it to my God in the great day, I dare not abandon my sentiments, or cease in all proper ways to propagate them.

"I, Mr. Chairman, have not desired, or asked any *compromise*. I have asked for nothing but to be protected in my rights as a citizen—rights which God has given me, and which are guaranteed to me by the constitution of my country. Have I, sir, been guilty of any infraction of the laws? Whose good name have I injured? When, and where, have I published any thing injurious to the reputation of Alton?

"Have I not, on the other hand, labored, in common with the rest of my fellow-citizens, to promote the reputation and interests of this City? What, sir, I ask, has been my offence? Put your finger upon it—define it—and I stand ready to answer for it. If I have committed any crime, you can easily convict me. You have public sentiment in your favor. You have (your) juries, and you have your attorney (looking at the attorney-general), and I have *no doubt* you can *convict* me. But if I have been guilty of no violation of law, why am I hunted up and down continually like a partridge upon the mountains? Why am I threatened with the *tar-barrel?* Why am I waylaid every day; and from night to night, and my life in jeopardy every hour?

"You have, sir, made up, as the lawyers say, a false issue; there are not two parties between whom there can be a *compromise*. I plant myself, sir, down on my unquestionable *rights*, and the question to be decided is, whether I shall be protected in the exercise and enjoyment of those rights,—*that is the question, sir;*—whether my property shall be protected; whether I shall be suffered to go home to my family at night without being assailed, and threatened with tar and feathers, and assassination; whether my afflicted wife, whose life has been in jeopardy, from continued alarm and excitement, shall, night after night, be driven from a sick-bed into the garret, to save her life from the brick-bats and violence of the mobs; *that, sir, is the question.*" Here, much affected and overcome by his feelings, he burst into tears. Many, not excepting even his enemies, wept—several sobbed aloud—and the sympathies of the whole meeting were deeply excited. He continued: "Forgive me, sir, that I have thus betrayed my weakness. It was the allusion to my family that overcame my feelings. Not, sir, I assure you, from any fears on my part. I have no personal fears. Not that I feel able to contest the matter with the whole community; I know perfectly well I am not. I know, sir, you can tar and feather me, hang me up, or put me into the Mississippi, without the least difficulty. But what then? Where shall I go? I have been made to feel that if I am not safe at Alton, I shall not be safe anywhere. I recently visited St. Charles to bring home my family, and was torn from their frantic embrace by a mob. I have been beset night and day at Alton. And now, if I leave here and go elsewhere, violence may overtake me in my retreat, and I have no more claim upon the protection of any other community than I have upon this; and I have concluded, after consultation with my friends, and earnestly seeking counsel of God, to remain at Alton, and here to insist on protection in the exercise of my rights. If the civil authorities refuse to protect me, I must look to God; and if I die, I have determined to make my grave in Alton."

CHAPTER XVIII.

The Riot of November 7th—Destruction of the fourth press—
The murder of Lovejoy—His funeral.

We have now arrived at the fatal night of the 7th of
Nov., 1837, and I give the details of the occurrences from
personal notes of my own. The fourth press had been
shipped to Alton from Cincinnati, and had been received
in the dead of the night (on the 6th)* by the friends of Mr.
Lovejoy, in presence of the mayor, and taken to its final
destination.

All was quiet in the City, and we considered the press
safe from harm, as it lay on storage with the most responsible and most respected firm in the city. No one had any
occasion to fear it, so quietly it lay in an upper loft, a mass
of iron boxed up, the innocent cause of so much bitter feeling. As night (of the 7th) approached, we gathered in the
building to talk over the situation, and congratulated each
other on peace. About nine o'clock, the company of men
began to disperse to their homes, when Mr. Gilman asked
if some few of the number would not volunteer to remain
through the night with him, for he intended staying as a

* When the press was received, on the night of the 6th, we were fully prepared to receive and defend it, having, in the building, about sixty men, well
armed and drilled, stationed on different floors in squads or companies of sufficient strength to do full execution if the mob should attempt to take the press
when landed from the boat. I have preserved one original order issued on
that night to the captain of one of these companies, by Orderly Sergt. J. W.
Chickering. And a fac-simile of the order is hereto attached.—H. T.

148

precaution in case the warehouse was attacked.   Nineteen
men answered the call, and the devoted little band prepared themselves for whatever might occur.   An hour had
elapsed before any signs of disturbance were noticed, but
then it was evident that a mob was gathering.   Messrs.
Keating and West asked permission to enter into the warehouse to confer with Mr. Gilman, and were incautiously
admitted by some one, who, in my opinion, was not possessed of much judgment, for they immediately discovered
the fact that there was a very small force inside, against
which to contend.

They informed us that unless the press was given up to
the gentlemen outside, the building would be burned over
our heads or blown up with powder.   We had, early in the
evening, selected for our captain, Enoch Long, who had
seen some service, thinking occasion might require con-
certed action on our part.   His method of defence was
much milder than some of us advocated, for we considered
it best to fire on the mob and make short work of it; but
he commanded that no one should shoot without his
order, an order which, from mistaken motives of mercy,
he hesitated to give until it was too late to intimidate the
besiegers.

The crowd gathered and attempted to force an entrance
into the building, but were temporarily checked in consequence of the order of our captain to one of his men to fire
upon them, in return for their shot which had entered the
building.   Our shot proved a fatal one: a man named
Bishop, one of the mob, was wounded and died before he
could be taken off from the ground.   The lull was a short

one: the mob returned, reinforced by ruffians who had been drinking to inspire themselves with courage, and with savage yells they shouted that they would "fire the building and shoot every d——d Abolitionist as he tried to make his escape!"   No orders were given us for any concentrated fire at any time; it was all hap-hazard, and every man did as he thought best.   At this juncture, the mayor appeared, and we asked him to lead us out to face the mob, and, if they would not disperse upon his command, that he should order us to fire upon them.   His answer was, that he had too much regard for our lives to do that,—but he, at the same time, most distinctly justified us in our defence. He attempted, afterward, to disperse them himself, but his power was gone—they merely laughed at his authority, as his weak and nerveless treatment of them, then and on former occasions of lawlessness, had destroyed all his influence as a magistrate.

Attempts were now made to fire the building, and against one side, in which there were no openings, a ladder was placed to reach the roof, on which a man ascended with a burning torch.   Captain Long called for volunteers to make a sortie, in order to prevent the accomplishment of their purpose, and Amos B. Roff, Royal Weller, and Elijah P. Lovejoy promptly stepped forth to execute his commission.   As they emerged from the building into the brilliant calm moonlight, shots were fired from behind a shelter, and five balls were lodged in the body of Mr. Lovejoy, others wounding Mr. Roff and Mr. Weller.   Mr. Lovejoy had strength enough to run back and up the stairs, crying out, as he went, "I am shot! I am shot! I am dead!"

When he reached the counting-room, he fell back into the arms of a bystander and was laid upon the floor, where he instantly passed away without a struggle and without speaking again.

Soon Messrs. Keating and West again approached the building, and informed Mr. Gilman that the roof was on fire, but that "the boys" would put it out if the press should be given up—that was all they wanted and nothing should be destroyed or any one harmed if the surrender were made. Mr. Gilman then, consulting with us all, said that there was property of great value on storage, and the interests of firms all over the State were represented there, that he felt great responsibility as Mr. Godfrey, his partner, was absent. To save these interests, he thought the building had better be abandoned and the press given up. Others coinciding in this opinion, it was decided to surrender the press, on condition that the mob would not attempt to enter the warehouse until we had left, and, further, that our departure should be without molestation. These terms being accepted, we secreted our arms and left the building together.

The dead body of Mr. Lovejoy and the two wounded men were guarded by S. J. Thompson, until after the mob entered. I remember, very well, delaying after the rest as I had an unusually good rifle, which I desired to place where the mob could not possibly discover it. I, thereby, escaped the risk the others ran of being shot, for no sooner had they left the building than the rioters broke their truce and fired more than a hundred bullets after them, but, owing to the slope of the ground, the shots passed harmlessly over their heads.

The friends then went sadly to their homes, thinking of the stain upon the fair name of their City, and the terrible injustice that was there being countenanced. The fire in the warehouse was extinguished, and the press was taken out and destroyed.

The next morning, we returned to where the dead body of Lovejoy lay, and removed it to his late home. His wife was absent at the house of a friend, so prostrated by the shock of these terrible events that her life was despaired of for many days. Owen Lovejoy received the corpse of his brother at the house, and preparations for the funeral, to take place the following day, where then made.

It was a rainy, depressing day, and I well remember now how Abram Breath, still a resident of Alton, and myself walked through mud and water, together, to the grave. We chafed in an angry mood as we thought of the silence then enforced upon us! The burial service was simple, consisting merely of prayers, by Mr. Lovejoy's constant friend, the Rev. Thomas Lippincott, no remarks being made, lest the mob should disturb the last sacred rites of our beloved friend. There had been no inquest over his body, no flowers were strewn upon his coffin. Mob-law not only reigned, but was insultingly triumphant.

It was thought that the silence of death, under such circumstances, well became the burial of liberty.

CHAPTER XIX.

The times and events—Letter from Winthrop S. Gilman, in whose warehouse the fourth press had been stored.

Mr. Winthrop S. Gilman, now of New York, has kindly contributed the following statement:

"HENRY TANNER, ESQ.—*Dear Sir:*—It is well known that in 1836, the Abolition of Slavery in the Southern States became a subject of intense feeling. The Southerners were a mighty power in Congress, of enormous wealth, dictatorial and proud. As the eyes of the Northern people opened to see the evils of slavery, they began to discuss the subject and to form Abolition societies. This, as is well known, provoked the hostility of the South, and the right of discussion, the right of petition on the subject, and the right of sending Abolition publications through the mails were denied.

"In the South, the people were heated and goaded on to madness by the cool interference of the North, with their peculiar institution. They were ready with fire and sword to persecute to death, and it became dangerous for a Northern man to travel there, unless he would yield to domination.

"In those days, Elijah P. Lovejoy suffered the loss of two or three printing-presses, at Alton, after having passed through the same trial with his St. Louis *Observer*, a Presbyterian newspaper, published first in St. Louis and afterwards at Alton. Lovejoy was a conscientious christian, an able writer, moderate in the expression of his views, but a perfect Martin Luther for firmness. His publications were objected to, by many Abolitionists, as of too mild a type. Slave-holders, on the other hand, demanded that there be no discussion of the dreaded topic; but he, fearless and conscientious, declined to banish the subject of slavery from his columns. The result of his labors was, that friends shipped him a new press, from Cincinnati, to take the place of the last, previously destroyed at Alton. They were determined that his mouth should not be gagged.

"I resided at Alton at that time, and knew Mr. Lovejoy well, though I was not a member of an Abolition society. I knew nothing of this fourth press, until after it was shipped, but opened our warehouse, at midnight, on the 6th of Nov., 1837, in presence of Hon. John M. Krum, the mayor of Alton,—a kindly and agreeable gentleman,—and had it snugly packed away in our third story, guarded by volunteer citizens with their guns.

"The mayor had been consulted by me and was present when the press was landed, and all arrangements were made, I believe, with his sanction. He told us he would make us all special constables, and would order us to fire on the mob, if we were assailed.

"The next day, I sent my wife, with her infant child, to Upper-Alton, to visit her father, and with about twenty armed men, only two or three of whom were Abolitionists, remained at the warehouse.

"The result is matter of history, and I will only add a

few details. We were assailed by a large mob on that bright moonlight night, with arms and hootings, with tin horns blowing and plenty of liquor flowing among them. A part of the mob filed in line on our river front and asked to speak with me. I stepped to the second-story door, and they demanded Lovejoy's press. I replied that we were there to defend it, and declined to give it up. One Carr, at the head of the column, raised his pistol to fire, when I was pulled away by my associates.

"Soon after this, the warehouse was fired upon, and the fire returned, and one of the mob, named Bishop, was killed. The rioters retired a while, but soon came on in new force, and placed a ladder against the side of the building in order to set fire to the roof. Lovejoy was then shot, but had strength to run up one flight of stairs and say, only, 'My God, I am shot!' Some of the defenders were wounded, and the roof of the warehouse was set on fire.

"Then Edward Keating, a lawyer, with one Henry West, came to ask a parley, and both were admitted. They, on behalf of the mob, offered a truce, on the basis of our not being fired upon, if we would leave the building; and that no property but the press should be destroyed. The choice being between two evils, *viz.:* the burning of our warehouse, with goods valued at many thousands of dollars,—some the property of third parties,—and the consequent destruction of the press; or, giving up the press, with an agreement that nothing else should be destroyed, and that we should not be fired upon when leaving the building, we accepted the latter alternative. An additional reason for this decision was the fact, that we had been in conflict about two hours, and the church-bell had been ringing,* but no help had come to us from the civil authorities, the majority of whom appeared to sympathize with the mob You, I recollect, bravely opposed this surrender, but were overruled.

"But what confidence can be placed in an agreement made by a mob? We *were* fired on, whilst leaving the building and the outlaws came in and made their gross remarks about the dead Lion, whose body then lay in our counting-room, and whose blood had consecrated the soil of Alton. Thus they 'strutted to their confusion,' pluming themselves on their triumph. Their eyes were holden that they could not see that Lovejoy's bed of shame was his real glory, and their exultations over him their deepest disgrace. One of the mob, a physician, offered his services to extract a ball from Mr. Weller, a member of our company, which offer, it is hardly necessary to say, was declined by him.

"So demoralized was the community by the influence of slavery that I was the only one (of a committee of citizens, appointed by a public meeting) that protested against resolutions which recommended Lovejoy to leave Alton. I contended that, as a citizen, he had rights which our community ought to protect. On that committee were the Hon. Cyrus Edwards, Hon. John Hogan, afterwards of St. Louis, and others. But what availed our defence of free-speech? Naught in the way of protecting the press. For

---

* It is an interesting fact, that Mrs. Graves, wife of the Presbyterian minister—a slender and delicate woman—opened the church, in her husband's absence, and rang the bell with all her strength.

had we then succeeded in beating off the mob, the return wave of frenzied, drunken rioters, with accessions from St. Louis, would, undoubtedly, have overcome us the next night.* But the value of the defence was enormously great, if we consider the advance of anti-slavery sentiment which it occasioned. Public meetings were held in the Northern States to condemn the murder of the first martyr in the cause of Abolition. Mr. Lovejoy was eulogized, as he deserved to be. The course taken by the defenders of free-speech was also highly commended.

"We can hardly realize now, how the sacrifices and patient sufferings and death of one man should influence society so largely. Then it was that Wendell Phillips, a young and comparatively unknown lawyer, made Faneuil Hall ring with his eloquence, thereby influencing many ardent patriots with a new zeal for the destruction of slavery. Then it was that Owen Lovejoy, who afterwards became the intrepid and able advocate of Abolition, in Congress, consecrated his life to the cause, in promoting which his brother had met his death.

"Then, also, was predicted the entire overthrow of a system of tyranny, which it took thirty years of discussion, persecution, violence, and war fully to terminate."

* As showing the spirit of the mob, at this time, reference is made to a fac-simile of a handbill, posted on my store door a few weeks after the trials in court were over, advertising fifty Black-Walnut Coffins for sale, this was occasioned because I had permitted a press to be established in one loft of my building, on which a small paper, called the *Altonian*, was published by Parks & Breath, good Abolitionists, as the times then went, but it was well known in the community that Rifles were kept for sale in that building, and the Coffins were not called for, they might have been needed had the mob called for that press.—H. T.

CHAPTER XX.

The voice of the contemporary press—In New York—In Massachusetts—In Pennsylvania—In Ohio—In Kentucky—In Missouri—In Tennessee—In Illinois.

I have stated in the preface, that no single event in the early history of the anti-slavery contest in the United States, produced a more profound impression, at the time, than did the martyrdom of Lovejoy. The remarks, quoted from John Quincy Adams and Dr. Channing, and the editorial article of the *Boston Recorder*, each implied that the burst of indignation from all parts of the land, as the result of this murder, was hardly exceeded by that which followed the battle of Lexington, in 1775.

I give below a few extracts, from newspapers, in different States, as specimens of the general utterances of the press:

NEW YORK.

From the *New-York Evening Post*, of Nov. 18, 1837:

"We cannot forbear expressing in the strongest language our condemnation of the manner in which the *Missouri Argus* speaks of this bloody event. The right to discuss freely and openly, by speech, by the pen, by the press, all political questions, and to examine and animadvert upon all political institutions, is a right, so clear and certain, so interwoven with our other liberties, so necessary in fact to their existence, that, without it, we must fall at once into despotism or anarchy. To say that he who holds unpopular opinions must hold them at the peril of his life, and that, if he expresses them in public, he has only himself to blame if they, who disagree with him, should rise and put him to death, is to strike at all rights, all liberties, all protection of law, and to justify or extenuate all crimes.

"We regard not this as a question connected with the Abolition of slavery, in the South, but as a question vital to the liberties of the entire Union. For our own part, we approve, we applaud, we would consecrate, if we could, to universal honor, the conduct of those who bled in this gallant defence of the freedom of the press. Whether they erred or not in their opinions, they did not err in the conviction of their right, as citizens of a democratic government, to express them, nor did they err in defending this right with an obstinacy which yielded only to death and the utmost violence."

From the *New-York American*, then edited by the late Hon. Charles King.

"American blood has been shed, at last, by American hands, employed to maintain slavery and crush free discussion,   *   *   *

"The town of Alton, as we have heretofore stated, is in the free-State of Illinois, on the Mississippi River, a few miles above St. Louis, where the law, concerning mobs, as pronounced by Judge Lawless, is that they are above and beyond its restraints.   *   *   *

"If this American blood—shed in the defence of the freedom of the press and the right of every American citizen to think, speak, and print his own honest opinions—be not signally vindicated, our representative institutions, our boasted freedom, our vaunted safety of property and life, will become, and deserves to become, the scoff and derision of the world."

MASSACHUSETTS.

From the *Boston Daily Advocate:*

"LIBERTY MURDERED.

"The horrid intelligence comes to us, from Illinois, that the Rev. Mr. Lovejoy has fallen a victim to the liberty of the press. Incarnate fiends and assassins have robbed a wife of a husband, children of a father, and society of a pure-minded man; for what? Because he stood under the shield of the Constitution, and defended the liberty of the press. A glorious cause to die in. Let his memory be embalmed. The blood of that innocent man will not sink into the ground. It will be required at the hands of all those who have raised that infernal spirit of mobism against free discussion and a free press."

From Wm. Lloyd Garrison's *Liberator.*

The *Liberator* was draped in mourning upon the receipt of the intelligence of Lovejoy's death. From the time the news reached Boston, the columns of that paper were crowded with notices of meetings, resolutions, speeches, extracts from other papers relating to this subject.

Particular accounts were given of a meeting of the Massachusetts Anti-Slavery Society, and of the great gathering, at which Dr. Channing's resolutions were adopted, in Faneuil Hall: also, a detailed account of a meeting, commemorative of Lovejoy, which was held December 22d, 1837 (Forefather's Day), in Boston, and of a similar one, held in the Broadway Tabernacle, in New York.

What Mr. Garrison wrote may be summed up in the

following sentence, taken from his editorial, in the issue of November 24th, 1837:

"LOVEJOY DIED THE REPRESENTATIVE OF PHILAN-THROPY AND JUSTICE, LIBERTY AND CHRISTIANITY: WELL, THEREFORE, MAY HIS FALL AGITATE ALL HEAV-EN AND EARTH."

PENNSYLVANIA.

From the *Philadelphia Observer:*

"ALTON MASSACRE.—The thrill of sensibility which seems to have been produced by the murder of Rev. E. P. Lovejoy, at Alton, has called forth, from every part of the land, a burst of indignation, which has not had its parallel, in this country, since the battle of Lexington, 1775.

"We devote a large space in our paper, to-day, to record the simultaneous burst of indignation, which this event has occasioned. One thing, which appears from looking over our exchange papers, has struck us with amazement, and that is, that the most decided expressions of disapproba-tion and abhorrence, of the deed, are from the slave-hold-ing States. With a large list of southern papers before us, we find not one attempt at an apology for the murderous outrage. The only apologists for it are found in our northern cities, and among editors, who have a circulation at the South, and some others, who have a pecuniary in-terest in retaining the favor of southern customers. What are we to infer from this fact?"

From the *Pittsburgh Times.*

"The Rev. Mr. Lovejoy has fallen a victim to the spirit of mobism, which is spreading itself more and more over the land. How long this lamentable state of things is to continue, Heaven only knows. How long, in this land of *liberty*, and of freedom of opinion, the knife of the assassin or the torch of the incendiary will be suffered to awe individuals, or frighten public sentiment, we can not pretend, with our short sight, to predict; but we believe we are borne out by the truth, in affirming that the Alton murder has made ten thousand accessions to the cause of Abolition. In this number, we do not include ourselves; but, although opposed to their cause, we are in favor of extending, to every portion of our fellow-citizens, the same right that we claim for ourselves, freedom of thought and the right of expressing our opinions."

OHIO.

From the *Painesville Republican:*

"This tragical event, the particulars of which will be found in another part of our paper, as given by the mayor, is one which calls for the severest reprehensions of every well-wisher to his country. It is an outrage, not only against the rights of individuals, but it is an open, high-handed attack on the freedom of speech and of the press, which is guaranteed to the people by the blood-bought charter of our liberties. We can hardly find language severe enough to express our utter abhorrence of such dastardly, wicked conduct—such a gross violation of those republican principles which ought to be held sacred by every son and daughter of Adam."

From the *Cincinnati Gazette:*

"ALTON,—ARSON,—AND MURDER.

"The mayor of Alton has issued a kind of extra-official

account of the arson and murder that recently occurred in that City. Its tone is very subdued, apologetical rather than otherwise.

"The measures taken, by the civil authority, appear to have been well calculated to encourage the violence they were directed to suppress. First, persuasion to those who were threatened—second, persuasion to the *Gentlemen Mobites?* Persuasion. When the mayor of a city undertakes to persuade a mob, he but invites them to proceed, with an almost positive assurance of impunity. We subjoin the mayor's statement, that our readers may judge for themselves."

From the *Cincinnati Journal*, whose editor was, from twelve to fourteen years a lawyer in Georgia:

"HORRID TRAGEDY.—The deed is done; the work is consummated. The Rev. E. P. Lovejoy is no more—he has died by the hands of a mob.

"*Have we nothing to do with slavery in a free-State?* Alas! slavery has something to do with us. Its fangs are upon us, rending our vitals. Talk of liberty in America? The poor privilege left us, in some parts of this fair land, is to be silent, to let the head, the heart, the tongue, the pen yield to the frantic spirit that riots unawed, unabashed. *Silence or death.* Alton! Alton!! we have heard of thy liberalities, of thy open-handed charity, of thy noble efforts in every good and benevolent enterprise. We loved thee for this, for this we honored thee, and thy fair fame was was borne on the breath of every wind, and men looked to Alton as the home of all that was excellent. Mobs have now made thee a by-word in the land—men hold in their breath when thy name strikes upon their ears. Thou art a polluted thing—blood is on thy garments.

"Liberty has found a grave in thy bosom. But hush— speak not—a mob is on the throne—the press must be dumb; for here, also, we have seen its riots."

KENTUCKY.

From the *Louisville Journal:*

"The Anti-Abolitionist, no less than the lover of his country and the detester of insubordination and crime, has cause deeply to regret this most atrocious tragedy.

"It is well if this martyrdom do not kindle up a flame which years, and all the efforts of the patriot, will scarce extinguish. Let those, who oppose the Abolitionists, take warning from this event, and let them ever remember that the only weapons with which these zealots can be success- fully encountered, are truth, reason, moderation, and toler- ance—and these are the only means to disarm them of their fanaticism; and that violence, outrage, and persecu- tion will infallibly inflame their zeal, enlarge their numbers, and increase the power of their dangerous doctrines."

From the *Louisville Herald:*

"Is a citizen of the United States to have his house— his castle—assailed by an armed mob, and is he to be mur- dered for defending the rights guaranteed to him by the constitution of his country? Are such things to be toler- ated, and will the presses of the country, which can find so much gall and wormwood, and so many maledictions for political opponents, pass by this outrage with a bare ex-

pression of cold regret? Are the *murderers*, for such we
pronounce them, to go unpunished? We trust not,—if
there is law in the land, we hope they will be made answer-
able to it,—if not, why then commend us to the despotism
of the Grand Turk, or the Czar, for they protect their people. The Mississippi, for a century to come, though it may
pour a constant flood, will not pour enough to wash out the
disgrace of the horrid murders of Alton, St. Louis, and
Vicksburgh."

MISSOURI.

From the *St. Louis Commercial Bulletin:*

"Be the offences of Lovejoy what they may, if he has
violated every law of the land, and outraged every feeling
of society, and every principle of moral and social duty—
the end of his unfortunate career—the mode and measure
of his punishment has changed the offender to a martyr,
and the presuming, daring sinner to an apostle of righteousness and a saint. His martyrdom will be celebrated by
every Abolitionist in the land, and the only consolation we
have is, that it was inflicted upon him in a non-slave-hold-
ing State."

TENNESSEE.

From the *Cumberland Presbyterian:*

"And what will European tyrants say to such conduct?
May they not, in scorn, point their slaves to the free institutions of America, and say, behold the workings of democratic principles; he that holds opinions, contrary to the
majority, must die the death. And shall American citizens boast of the freedom of the press, when he who dares
to express his sentiments, does it at the hazard of his life;

the gag-laws of Europe are mildness itself, compared to the bloody tragedy at Alton.

"And surely the honor of our country, the cause of justice, the liberty of the nation, loudly demands that the perpetrators of this foul deed shall be dealt with by the laws of the land in the severest manner, consistent with justice. The honor of republican governments, the vindication of the character of these United States loudly call upon the civil authorities, of Illinois, to see to it, that the murderers of Rev. E. P. Lovejoy shall be brought to condign punishment."

ILLINOIS.

From the *Peoria Register*:

"We have heard the names* of some of the gallant party who defended the warehouse, and they are the men who, for the last three years, by their christian philanthropy and public and private enterprise, have given to Alton the high character which the entire West has awarded her. The floating population, which they had invited thither—to whom they had given employment—

---

* I herewith append the names of all, and so far as known if living and where, or if known to be dead—and I believe no evil reports (saving the indictment alluded to in this book) have been brought against the names of any of them. The names of the twenty men, that night in the building, are as follows:

ELIJAH P. LOVEJOY, killed by the mob, Nov. 7, 1837.

AMOS B. ROFF, then wounded, since dead.

ROYAL WELLER, then wounded, since dead.

WILLIAM HARNED, dead.

JAMES MORSE, JR., dead.

JOHN S. NOBLE, dead.

EDWARD BREATH, (subsequently missionary to Persia), dead.

have become the assassins of the character of the City, and the murderers of one of her citizens.

"We can not use smooth phrases in speaking of these enormities. Is human life to be held merely at the caprice of the rabble?

"Was it for this, our fathers periled their lives and fortunes to effect our national independence? Better had it been to have remained the subjects of a foreign government, which would have secured to each protection of *life and law*, than to have left these dearest rights of man to the tender mercies of a licentious mob."

GEO. H. WALWORTH, dead.

J. C. WOODS, dead.

GEO. H. WHITNEY, dead.

REUBEN GERRY, dead.

WINTHROP S. GILMAN, living in New-York City.

ENOCH LONG, living in Sabula, Iowa.

GEORGE T. BROWN, living in Alton, Ill.

SAMUEL J. THOMPSON, died before 1841.

H. D. DAVIS, do not know if living or dead.

D. F. RANDALL, do not know if living or dead.

D. BURT LOOMIS, residence unknown.

THADDEUS B. HURLBUT, residence, Upper-Alton.

HENRY TANNER, Buffalo, N. Y.

CHAPTER XXI.

Dr. Channing's address to the citizens of Boston.

From the *New York American*, of 5th Dec., 1837:

"I feel that I owe to my fellow-citizens and myself, to offer some remarks on the proceedings of the Board of Aldermen, in relation to a petition presented to them for the use of Faneuil Hall, in order that there might be an expression of public sentiment in regard to the late ferocious assault on the liberty of the press at Alton. Had I for a moment imagined, that by placing my name at the head of this petition, I' was to bring myself before the public as I have done, I should have been solicitous to avoid the distinction.

"But the past can not be recalled; and having performed this act from a conviction of duty, I can not regret it. My only desire is, that its true character may be understood 'by my fellow-citizens, who will not, I believe, when they know the truth, give the sanction of their approbation to the proceedings of the government.

"The petition was as follows:

"'BOSTON, Nov. 27th, 1837.

"'*To the Mayor and Aldermen of the City of Boston:*

"'The undersigned, citizens of Boston, request that the use of Faneuil Hall may be granted to them on Monday evening, Dec. 4th, for the purpose of holding a public meeting, to notice, in a suitable manner, the recent murder in the city of Alton, of a native of New England and a citizen of the free-State of Illinois, who fell in defence of the freedom of the press.'"

"This petition was rejected by the Board of Aldermen, on the ground that the resolutions which might be passed at the proposed meeting, would not express the public opinion of the City, and would even create a disgraceful confusion in Faneuil Hall, or, in other words, would excite a mob. I need not say to those who know me, that I am incapable of proposing a measure which would seem to me fitted to expose the City to tumult. The truth is, that the possibility of such an occurrence did not enter my thoughts. The object of the proposed meeting was so obvious, so unexceptionable, so righteous, and had such claims on every friend of order and liberty, that I did not pause a moment when I was requested to sign the petition. I should have pronounced it impossible that a man of common sense and common honesty could view and pass over the tragedy of Alton, as a matter touching merely the interests of one or another party. To me it had a character of its own, which stood out in terrible relief. I saw in it systematic, deliberate murder, for the destruction of the freedom of the press. The petition was presented for one purpose and one only, namely, that the good people of Boston might manifest, in the most solemn and impressive manner, their deep abhorrence of the spirit of mobs, which threatens all our institutions, and particularly might express their utter, uncompromising reprobation of the violence which has been offered to the freedom of speech and press.

"The Freedom of the Press, the sacredness of this right,

—the duty of maintaining it against all assaults,—this was the great idea to which the meeting was intended to give utterance. I was requested to prepare the resolutions, and I was meditating this work when I heard the decision of the Board of Aldermen. My single aim was, to frame such resolutions as should pledge all who should concur in them to the exertion of their whole influence for the suppression of mobs, for the discouragement of violence, for the vindication of the supremacy of the laws, and especially for the assertion and defence of the freedom of the press. My intention was, to exclude all reference to parties, all topics about which there could be a division among the friends of liberty. No other resolutions could have been drawn up in consistency with the petition; and the Board of Aldermen had no right to expect any others. To intimate, that such resolutions would not express the public opinion of Boston, and would even create a mob, is to pronounce the severest libel on the City. It is to assert that peaceful citizens can not meet here in safety to strengthen and pledge themselves against violence and in defence of the dearest and most sacred rights. And has it come to this? Has Boston fallen so low? May not its citizens be trusted to come together to express the great principles of liberty, for which their fathers died? Are our fellow-citizens to be *murdered* in the act of defending their property and of asserting the right of free discussion; and is it unsafe in this metropolis, once the refuge of liberty, to express abhorrence of the deed? If such be our degradation, we ought to know the awful truth; and those among us who retain a portion of the spirit of our ancestors, should set themselves to work to recover their degenerate posterity. But I do not believe in this degeneracy. The people of Boston may be trusted. There is a moral soundness in this community on the great points involved in the petition which has been rejected. There is among us a deep abhorrence of the spirit of violence which is spreading through our land; and from this City there ought to go forth a voice to awaken the whole country to its danger, to the growing peril of the substitution of lawless force for the authority of the laws. This in truth was the great object of those who proposed the meeting, to bring out a loud general expression of opinion and feeling, which would awe the spirit of mobs, and would especially secure the press from violence. Instead of this, what is Boston now doing? Into what scale is the City now thrown? Boston now says to Alton, go on; destroy the press; put down the liberty of speech; and still more, murder the citizens who assert it; and no united voice shall here be lifted up against you, lest a like violence should break forth among ourselves.

"It is this view of the rejection of the petition which deeply moves me. That a petition, bearing my name, should be denied, would not excite a moment's thought or feeling. But that this City, which I have been proud to call my home, should be so exhibited to the world, and should exert this disastrous influence on the country, this I can not meet with indifference.

"I earnestly hope that my fellow-citizens will demand the public meeting which has been refused, with a voice which can not be denied; but unless so called, I do not desire that it should be held. If not demanded by acclamation, it would very possibly become a riot. A government which announces its expectation of a mob, does virtually, though unintentionally, summon a mob, and would then cast all the blame of it on the "rash men" who might become its victims.

"But is there no part of our country, where a voice of power shall be lifted up in defence of rights incomparably more precious than the temporary interests which have often crowded Faneuil Hall to suffocation? Is the whole country asleep? An event has occurred, which ought to thrill the hearts of this people as the heart of one man.

"A martyr has fallen among us to the freedom of the press. A citizen has been *murdered* in defence of the right of free discussion. I do not ask whether he was Christian or unbeliever, whether he was Abolitionist or Colonizationist. He has been murdered in exercising what I hold to be the dearest right of the citizen. Nor is this a solitary act of violence. It is the consummation of a long series of assaults on public order, on freedom, on the majesty of the laws. I ask, is there not a spot in the country whence a voice of moral reprobation, of patriotic remonstrance, of solemn warning, shall go forth to awaken the slumbering community? There are indeed, in various places, meetings of Anti-Slavery Societies to express their sorrow for a fallen brother. But in these I take no part. What I desired was, that the citizens of Boston, of all parties, should join as one man in putting down the reign of terror by the force of opinion; and in spreading a shield over our menaced liberties, I felt that the very fact that the majority of the people here, are opposed to the peculiar opinions of our murdered fellow-citizen, would give increased authority to our condemnation of this ferocious deed.

"The principles on which I have acted in this affair, are such as have governed my whole life. This is not the first time in which I have come forward to defend the freedom of opinion, the freedom of speech, the freedom of the press. Not a few of my fellow-citizens will bear witness to the sincerity of my devotion to this cause. The rights of a human being to inquire, to judge, and to express his honest conviction, these are dear to me as life; and if I ask a distinction in society, it is that of being a defender of these. I can not, I will not, tamely and silently, see these trampled down in the person of a fellow-citizen, be he rich or poor, be he friend or foe, be he the advocate or the opposer of what I deem the truth.

"That in these sentiments I have the sympathy of my fellow-citizens, I can not doubt. I am confident, that, when the true import of the petition which I have signed is understood, the vast majority will agree with me in the fitness of the action which it was intended to promote. I have no distrust of my fellow-citizens. They are true to the principles of liberty; and the time, I hope, is near, when the stain, now thrown on our ancient and free City, will be wiped away, when a petition, headed by a worthier name, will assemble the wise and good, the friends of order and liberty, of all sects and parties, to bear their solemn testimony against the spirit of misrule and violence, to express their devotion to the laws, and their unconquerable purpose to maintain the freedom of speech and of the press.   "WM. E. CHANNING."

CHAPTER XXII.

The maiden speech of Wendell Phillips in Faneuil Hall, Boston.

Rev. William Ellery Channing, D.D., headed a petition to the Mayor and Aldermen of Boston, asking the use of Faneuil Hall for a public meeting. It was thought that the spot designated "The Cradle of Liberty," where patriotic men had so often met during the struggle of the colonies with the mother country, was the only fitting place for such a meeting. But the influence of slavery among politicians was so great that for a time the use of the hall was refused. Dr. Channing then addressed a very impressive letter to his fellow-citizens, which resulted in a meeting of influential Bostonians at the Old Court Room, where resolutions in favor of the meeting were unanimously adopted and measures were taken to secure a much greater array of names to the petition. This call, the Mayor and Aldermen felt constrained to obey.

The great meeting was held on the 8th of December, 1837, with the Hon. Jonathan Phillips, kinsman of Wendell Phillips who was then a young lawyer, in the chair.

Dr. Channing made a brief and eloquent address. Resolutions, drawn by him, were then read and offered by Mr. Hallett, and seconded in an able speech by George S. Hillard, Esq. The Hon. James T. Austin, Attorney-General of the Commonwealth, followed in a speech of the utmost bitterness, styled by the *Boston Atlas*, a few days after, "most able and triumphant." He compared the slaves to a menagerie of wild beasts, and the rioters at Alton to the "orderly mob" which threw the tea overboard in 1773, talked of the "conflict of laws" between Missouri and Illinois, declared that Lovejoy was "presumptuous and imprudent," and "died as the fool' dieth"; in direct and most insulting reference to Dr. Channing, he asserted that a clergyman with a gun in his hand, or one "mingling in the debates of a popular assembly, was marvelously out of place."

The speech of the Attorney-General produced great excitement throughout the Hall. Wendell Phillips, now so celebrated for his eloquence, who had not expected to take part in the meeting, rose to reply.

That portion of the assembly which sympathized with Mr. Austin now became so boisterous, that Mr. Phillips had difficulty for a while in getting the attention of the audience. Opposition, bluster, and noise, had, however, no other effect upon this young man than to inspire his eloquence. Knowing full well that the official who had preceded him was faithless to those principles which had made the name of Faneuil Hall illustrious, he boldly condemned the Attorney-General's remarks in the following pungent and most eloquent address, which took the audience by storm:

"Mr. Chairman:—We have met for the freest discussion of these resolutions, and the events which gave rise to them. [Cries of 'Question,' 'Hear him,' 'Go on,' 'No gagging,' etc.]

"I hope I shall be permitted to express my surprise at the sentiments of the last speaker,—surprised not only at such sentiments from such a man, but at the applause they have received within these walls. A comparison has been drawn between the events of the Revolution and the tragedy at Alton. We have heard it asserted here, in Faneuil Hall, that Great Britain had a right to tax the Colonies, and we have heard the mob at Alton, the drunken murderers of Lovejoy, compared to those patriot fathers who threw the tea overboard! [Great applause.] Fellow-citizens, is this Faneuil-Hall doctrine? ['No, no.'] The mob at Alton were met to wrest from a citizen his just rights,—met to resist the laws. We have been told that our fathers did the same; and the glorious mantle of Revolutionary precedent has been thrown over the mobs of our day. To make out their title to such defence, the gentleman says, that the British Parliament had a *right* to tax these Colonies. It is manifest that, without this, his parallel falls to the ground; for Lovejoy had stationed himself within constitutional bulwarks. He was not only defending the freedom of the press, but he was under his own roof, in arms with the sanction of the civil authority. The men who assailed him went against and over the laws. The *mob*, as the gentleman terms it,—mob, forsooth! certainly we sons of the tea-spillers are a marvelously patient generation!—the 'orderly mob' which assembled in the Old South to destroy the tea, were met to resist, not the laws, but illegal exactions. Shame on the American who calls the tea-tax and stamp-act *laws!* Our fathers resisted, not the king's prerogative, but the king's usurpation. To find any other account, you must read our Revolutionary history upside down. Our State archives are loaded with arguments of John Adams, to prove the taxes laid by the British Parliament unconstitutional,—beyond its power. It was not till this was made out that the men of New England rushed to arms. The arguments of the Council Chamber and the House of Representatives preceded and sanctioned the contest. To draw the conduct of our ancestors into a precedent for mobs, for a right to resist laws we ourselves have enacted, is an insult to their memory· The difference between the excitements of those days and our own, which the gentleman in kindness to the latter has overlooked, is simply this: the men of that day went for the right, as secured by the laws. They were the people rising to sustain the laws and constitution of the Province. The rioters of our day go for their own wills, right or wrong. Sir, when I heard the gentleman lay down principles which place the murderers of Alton side by side with Otis and Hancock, with Quincy and Adams, I thought those pictured lips [pointing to the portraits in the Hall] would have broken into voice to rebuke the recreant American—the slanderer of the dead—[Great applause and counter applause.] The gentleman said that he should sink into insignificance if he dared to gainsay the principles of these resolutions. Sir, for the sentiments he has uttered, on soil consecrated by the prayers of Puritans and the blood of patriots, the earth should have yawned and swallowed him up. [Applause and hisses, with cries of 'Take that back.' The uproar became so great that for a long time no one could be heard. At length, G. Bond, Esq., and Hon. W. Sturgis, came to Mr. Phillips' side at the front of the platform. They were met with cries of

'Phillips or nobody,' 'Make him take back 'recreant',' 'He sha'n't go on till he takes it back.' When it was understood they intended to sustain, not to interrupt, Mr. Phillips.]   Mr. Sturgis was listened to, and said: 'I did not come here to take any part in this discussion, nor do I intend to; but I entreat you, fellow-citizens, by every thing you hold sacred,—I conjure you by every association connected with this Hall, consecrated by our fathers to freedom of discussion,—that you listen to every man who addresses you in a decorous manner.' Mr. Phillips resumed: "Fellow-citizens, I can not take back my words. Surely the Attorney-General, so long and well known here, needs not the aid of your hisses against one so young as I am,—my voice never before heard within these walls! Another ground has been taken to excuse the mob, and throw doubt and discredit on the conduct of Lovejoy and his associates.   Allusion has been made to what lawyers understand very well,—'the conflict of laws.' We are told that nothing but the Mississippi River rolls between St. Louis and Alton, and the conflict of laws somehow or other gives the citizens of the former a right to find fault with the defender of the press for publishing his opinions so near their limits. Will the gentleman venture that argument before lawyers? How the laws of the two States could be said to come into conflict in such circumstances, I question whether any lawyer in this audience can explain or understand.

"No matter whether the line that divides one sovereign State from another be an imaginary one or ocean-wide, the moment you cross it the State you leave is blotted out of existence, so far as you are concerned. The Czar might as well claim to control the deliberations of Faneuil Hall, as the laws of Missouri demand reverence, or the shadow of obedience, from an inhabitant of Illinois.

"I must find some fault with the statement which has been made of the events at Alton. It has been asked why Lovejoy and his friends did not appeal to the executive,—trust their defence to the police of the City. It has been hinted that, from hasty and ill-judged excitement, the men within the building provoked a quarrel, and that he fell in the course of it, one mob resisting another.

"Recollect, Sir, that they did act with the approbation and sanction of the Mayor. In strict truth, there was no executive to appeal to for protection. The Mayor acknowledged that he could not protect them. They asked him if it was lawful for them to defend themselves. He told them it was, and sanctioned their assembling in arms to do so. They were not, then, a mob; they were not merely citizens defending their own property; they were in some sense the *posse comitatus*, adopted for the occasion into the police of the City, acting under the order of a magistrate. It was civil authority resisting lawless violence. Where then, was the imprudence? Is the doctrine to be sustained here, that it is *imprudent* for men to aid magistrates in executing the laws?

"Men are continually asking each other, had Lovejoy a right to resist? Sir, I protest against the question, instead of answering it. Lovejoy did not resist, in the sense they mean. He did not throw himself back on the natural right of self-defence.

"He did not cry anarchy, and let slip the dogs of civil war, careless of the horrors which would follow.

"Sir, as I understand this affair, it was not an individual protecting his property; it was not one body of armed men resisting another, and making the streets of a peaceful city run blood with their contentions. It did not bring back the scenes in some old Italian cities, where family met family, and faction met faction, and mutually trampled the laws under foot.

"No; the men in that house were regularly *enrolled*, under the sanction of the Mayor. There being no militia in Alton, about seventy men were enrolled, with the approbation of the Mayor. These relieved each other every other night. About thirty men were in arms on the night of the sixth, when the press was landed. The next evening, it was not thought necessary to summon more than half that number; among these was Lovejoy. It was, therefore, you perceive, Sir, the police of the city resisting rioters,—civil government breasting itself to the shock of lawless men.

"Here is no question about the right of self-defence. It is in fact simply this : Has the civil magistrate a right to put down a riot?

"Some persons seem to imagine that anarchy existed at Alton from the commencement of these disputes. Not at all. 'No one of us,' says an eye-witness and a comrade of Lovejoy, 'has taken up arms during these disturbances but at the command of the Mayor.'

"Anarchy did not settle down on that devoted City till Lovejoy breathed his last. Till then the law, represented in his person, sustained itself against its foes. When he fell, civil authority was trampled under foot. He had 'planted himself on his constitutional rights'—appealed to the laws,—claimed the protection of the civil authority, —taken refuge under 'the broad shield of the constitution. When through that he was pierced and fell, he fell but one sufferer in a common catastrophe.' He took refuge under the banner of liberty,—amid its folds; and when he fell, its glorious stars and stripes, the emblem of free institutions, around which cluster so many heart-stirring memories, were blotted out in the Martyr's blood. It has been stated, perhaps inadvertently, that Lovejoy or his comrades fired first. This is denied by those who have the best means of knowing. Guns were first fired by the mob. After being twice fired on, those within the building consulted together and deliberately returned the fire. But suppose they did fire first. They had a right so to do; not only the right which every citizen has to defend himself, but the further right which every civil officer has to resist violence. Even if Lovejoy fired the first gun, it would not lessen his claim to our sympathy, or destroy his title to be considered a martyr in defence of a free press. The question now is, Did he act within the Constitution and the laws?

"The men who fell in State Street, on the 5th of March, 1770, did more than Lovejoy is charged with. They were the *first* assailants. Upon some slight quarrel they pelted the troops with every missile within reach. Did this bate one jot of the eulogy with which Hancock and Warren hallowed their memory, hailing them as the first martyrs in the cause of American liberty? If, Sir, I had adopted what are called Peace principles, I might lament the circumstances of this case. But all you who believe, as I do, in the right and duty of magistrates to execute the laws, join with me and brand as base hypocrisy the conduct of those who assemble, year after year, on the 4th of July, to fight over the battles of the Revolution, and yet 'damn with faint praise,' or load with obloquy the memory of this man, who shed his blood in defence of life, liberty, property, and the freedom of the press!

"Throughout that terrible night, I find nothing to regret but this, that within the limits of our country, civil authority should have been so prostrated as to oblige a citizen to arm in his own defence, and to arm in vain.

"The gentleman says, Lovejoy was presumptuous and imprudent,—he 'died as the fool dieth.'

And a reverend gentleman* of the city, tells us that no citizen has a right to publish opinions disagreeable to the community. If any mob follows such publication, on *him* rests its guilt! He must wait, forsooth, till the people come up to it and agree with him! This libel on liberty goes on to say, that the want of right to speak as we think is an evil inseparable from republican institutions! If this be so, what are they worth? Welcome the despotism of the Sultan, where one knows what he may publish and what he may not, rather than the tyranny of this many-headed monster, the mob, where we know not what we

---

* See Rev. Hubbard Winslow's discourse on *Liberty!* in which he defines "republican liberty" to be "liberty to say and do what the *prevailing* voice and will of the brotherhood will allow and protect."

may do or say, till some fellow-citizen has tried it, and paid for the lesson with his life.   This clerical absurdity chooses, as a check for the abuses of the press, not the *law*, but the dread of a mob.   By so doing, it deprives not only the individual and the minority of their rights, but the majority also, since the expression of *their* opinion may sometimes provoke disturbance from the minority.   A few men may make a mob as well as many.   The majority, then, have no right, as Christian men, to utter their sentiments, if by any possibility it may lead to a mob!   Shades of Hugh Peters and John Cotton, save us from such pulpits!

"*Imprudent* to defend the liberty of the press!   Why? Because the defence was unsuccessful?   Does success gild crime into patriotism, and the want of it change heroic self-devotion to imprudence?   Was Hampden imprudent when he drew the sword and threw away the scabbard? Yet he, judged by that single hour, was unsuccessful. After a short exile, the race he hated sat again upon the throne.

"Imagine yourself present when the first news of Bunker Hill battle reached a New-England town.   The tale would have run thus: 'The patriots are routed,—the red-coats victorious,—Warren lies dead upon the field.'   With what scorn would that *Tory* have been received, who should have charged Warren with *imprudence!*   Who should have said that, bred a physician, he was 'out of place' in that battle, and 'died as the *fool dieth*'!   [Great applause.] How would the intimation have been received, that Warren and his associates should have waited a better time? But if success be indeed the only criterion of prudence, *Respice finem*,—wait till the end.

"*Presumptuous* to assert the freedom of the press on American ground! Is the assertion of such freedom before the age? So much before the age as to leave one no right to make it because it displeases the community? Who invents this libel on his country? It is the very thing which entitles Lovejoy to greater praise.

"The disputed right which provoked the Revolution— taxation without representation—is far beneath that for which he died. [Here there was a strong and general expression of disapprobation.] One word, gentlemen. As much as *thought* is better than money, so much is the cause in which Lovejoy died nobler than a mere question of taxes. James Otis thundered in this Hall when the king did but touch his *pocket*. Imagine, if you can, his indignant eloquence, had England offered to put a gag upon his lips. [Great applause.] The question that stirred the Revolution touched our civil interests. *This* concerns us not only as citizens, but as immortal beings. Wrapped up in its fate, saved or lost with it, are not only the voice of the statesman, but the instructions of the pulpit, and the progress of our faith.

"The clergy 'marvelously out of place' where free speech is battled for,—liberty of speech on national sins? Does the gentleman remember that freedom to preach was first gained, dragging in its train freedom to print?

"I thank the clergy here present, as I reverence their predecessors, who did not so far forget their country in their immediate profession as to deem it duty to separate themselves from the struggle of '76,—the Mayhews and Coopers, who remembered they were citizens before they were clergymen.

"Mr. Chairman, from the bottom of my heart I thank that brave little band at Alton for resisting. We must remember that Lovejoy had fled from city to city,—suffered the destruction of three presses patiently. At length he took counsel with friends, men of character, of tried integrity, of wide views, of Christian principle.

"They thought the crisis had come; it was full time to assert the laws. They saw around them, not a community like our own, of fixed habits, of character moulded and settled, but one 'in the gristle, not yet hardened into the bone of manhood.' The people there, children of our older States, seem to have forgotten the blood-tried principles of their fathers the moment they lost sight of our New-England hills. Something was to be done to show them the priceless value of the freedom of the press, to bring back and set right their wandering and confused ideas. He and his advisers looked out on a community, staggering like a drunken man, indifferent to their rights and confused in their feelings. Deaf to argument, haply they might be stunned into sobriety. They saw that of which we can not judge, the *necessity* of resistance. Insulted law called for it. Public opinion fast hastening on the downward course, must be arrested. Does not the event show they judged rightly? Absorbed in a thousand trifles, how has the nation all at once come to a stand? Men begin, as in 1776 and 1640, to discuss principles, to weigh characters, to find out where they are. Haply we may awake before we are borne over the precipice.

"I am glad, Sir, to see this crowded house. It is good for us to be here. When Liberty is in danger, Faneuil Hall has the right, it is her duty, to strike the key-note for these United States. I am glad, for one reason, that remarks, such as those to which I have alluded, have been uttered here. The passage of these resolutions, in spite of this opposition led by the Attorney-General of the Common-wealth, will show more clearly, more decisively, the deep indignation with which Boston regards this outrage."

CHAPTER XXIII.

The Alton Trials—Action of the Grand Jury—Indictment of the protectors of the press—A remarkable document—Defence by George T. M. Davis—Acquittal—Indictment of the Rioters—Their acquittal—Conclusion.

This chapter in American history would be incomplete without an outline of the trials which were instituted in Alton, immediately after the death of Lovejoy.

We were under the practice of the "New Code" of Judge Lawless, which justified mobs in cases where the multitude had been "*seized upon and impelled by that mysterious, metaphysical, and almost electric frenzy, which in all ages and nations has hurried on the infuriated multitude to deeds of death and destruction.*" Action under the "New Code" had culminated in the "death" of a perfectly innocent and law-abiding citizen, and in the "destruction" of his property. But notwithstanding the "electric frenzy," it appeared clear that some one had violated the majesty of law in Alton, and that that majesty needed to be vindicated. It was quite natural, therefore, that when the Grand Jury met, with Thomas G. Hawley, as foreman,* it should find the following indictment:

* The following named persons composed the jury:

THOMAS G. HAWLEY,	JOHN W. BUFFUM,
WILLIAM ARUNDELL,	SAMUEL C. PIERCE,
JOHN H. COOK,	M. H. CARROLL,
WILLIAM HAYDEN,	GEORGE WENT,
WILLIAM L. WILCOX,	GEORGE MCBRIDE,

187

"Of the January Term of the Municipal Court of the City of Alton, in the year of our Lord one thousand eight hundred and thirty-eight.

"STATE OF ILLINOIS, ⎱ SS.:
   CITY OF ALTON, ⎰

"The Grand Jurors chosen, selected, and sworn, in and for the body of the City of Alton, in the County of Madison, in the name and by the authority of the People of the State of Illinois, upon their oaths, present that Enoch Long, Amos B. Roff, George H. Walworth, George H. Whitney, William Harned, John S. Noble, James Morse, Jr., Henry Tanner, Royal Weller, Reuben Gerry, Thaddeus B. Hurlbut, and Winthrop S. Gilman, all late of the City of Alton, in the County of Madison, and State of Illinois, on the seventh day of November, in the year of our Lord one thousand eight hundred and thirty-seven, with force and arms, at the City of Alton, aforesaid, and within the corporate limits of said City, unlawfully, riotously, and routously, and in a violent and tumultuous manner, resisted and opposed an attempt, then and there being made, to break up and destroy a printing-press, then and there being found, the goods and chattels of Benjamin Godfrey and Winthrop S. Gilman, and then being in their possession, contrary to the form of the statute, in such

THOMAS P. WOOLRIDGE,	WILLIAM RICE,
JOHN QUIGLEY,	WALTER SCHIELDS,
ELI McGUNNEGLE,	CHARLES J. BARRY,
THOMAS STANTON,	REUBEN REYNOLDS,
WILLIAM DAWES,	JOHN HENDRICKSON,
DANIEL BRAYWELL,	JOHN McGUIRE.

cases made and provided, and against the peace and dignity of the people of the State of Illinois.

"And the Jurors aforesaid, in the name, and by the authority aforesaid, upon their oaths aforesaid, do further present, that Enoch Long, Amos B. Roff, George H. Walworth, George H. Whitney, William Harned, John S. Noble, James Morse, Jr., Henry Tanner, Royal Weller, Reuben Gerry, Thaddeus B. Hurlbut, and Winthrop S. Gilman, all late of the City of Alton, in the County of Madison, and State of Illinois, on the seventh day of November, in the year of our Lord one thousand eight hundred and thirty-seven, with force and arms, at the City of Alton, aforesaid, and within the corporate limits of said City, unlawfully, riotously, routously, and in a violent and tumultuous manner, defended and resisted an attempt, then and there being made, by divers persons, to the jurors aforesaid unknown, to force open and enter the storehouse of Benjamin Godfrey and Winthrop S. Gilman, there situate, contrary to the form of the statute, in such case made and provided, and against the peace and dignity of the People of the State of Illinois.

"FRANCIS B. MURDOCK,

"Prosecuting Attorney for the Municipal Court of the City of Alton.

"Endorsed upon the back, 'A true bill.'

"THOMAS G. HAWLEY, Foreman."

It is true, that these gentlemen, thus indicted, whilst quietly resting for the night, had been attacked in their own castle, and had made no defence, until a mob, threatening their lives, had attempted to break in the doors.

But, it is very plain, also, that according to the "New Code," they had violated law, by resisting "the electric frenzy of the infuriated multitude," which only threatened their lives, because they had refused to surrender their property. George T. M. Davis, Esq., now of the City of New York, was then one of the most prominent members of the bar in Illinois, with a very large and exacting business on his hands. He saw the unrighteousness of these charges, and immediately tendered his valuable service, free of charge, to the defenders of the press.

When the trial came on, January 17, 1838, he moved the Court that a separate trial be granted Winthrop S. Gilman, alleging, that in no way could he so well show how utterly devoid Mr. Gilman was of any criminal intent, as by a separate trial.

The motion was granted. About sixty of those in sympathy with the mob prayed the Court that U. F. Linder, who was at that time Attorney-General, and whose associations and abilities peculiarly fitted him for the work of a criminal lawyer, in such a case as this, might be permitted to assist the attorney for the Municipal Court of Alton, and this petition was also granted.

Without troubling the reader with any details of a long and tedious trial, in which the truth came out very clearly, that every act of Mr. Gilman, and his associates, was performed with the concurrence of the Mayor, and, as those gentlemen supposed, with the authority of law; and after a very able argument by Mr. Davis, and his associate counsel, Hon. Alfred Cowles, Mr. Gilman was pronounced not guilty.

The names of the men composing the jury were: James S. Stone, Timothy Terrel, Stephen Griggs, Effingham Cock, George Allcorn, Peter Whittaker, Horace W. Buffum, Washington Libbey, Luther Johnson, George L. Ward, Anthony Olney, and Jacob Rice.

The Attorney-General plied his vocation to make the wrong appear the right, but it was all in vain.

Mr. Gilman's course being thus triumphantly vindicated, the City Attorney entered a *nolle prosequi* in the cases of his associates.

With the true spirit of compromise, characteristic so often of men of no fixed principle, the Alton Grand Jury had also indicted eleven of the ringleaders of the mob, as shown by the following indictment:

"Of the January Term of the Municipal Court, of the City of Alton, in the year of our Lord one thousand eight hundred and thirty-eight.

"STATE OF ILLINOIS, ⎫ ss.:
   CITY OF ALTON, ⎭

"The Grand Jurors, chosen, selected, and sworn, in and for the body of the City of Alton, in the County of Madison, in the name, and by the authority, of the people of the State of Illinois, upon their oaths, present that John Solomon, Solomon Morgan, Levi Palmer, Horace Beall, Josiah Nutter, James Jennings, Jacob Smith, David Butler, William Carr, James M. Rock, and Frederick Bruchy, all late of the City of Alton, in the County of Madison, and State of Illinois, on the 7th day of November, in the year of our Lord one thousand eight hundred and thirty-seven, with force and arms, at the City of Alton, aforesaid, and within the corporate limits of said City, unlawfully, and with force and violence, did enter the storehouse of Benjamin Godfrey and Winthrop S. Gilman, there situate, and one printing-press, the property, goods, and chattels of the said Benjamin Godfrey and Winthrop S. Gilman, then and there being found, did, unlawfully, riotously, and with force and violence, break and destroy, contrary to the form of the statute, in such cases made and provided, and against the peace and dignity of the people of the State of Illinois.

"FRANCIS B. MURDOCK,

"Prosecuting Attorney for the Municipal Court of the
City of Alton.

"Endorsed, 'A true bill.'

"THOMAS G. HAWLEY, Foreman."

The names of the jurors who tried the eleven men named in the foregoing indictment, were: Timothy Terrell, John P. Ash, William S. Gaskins, George Allcorn, John Clark, William T. Hankinson, Richard P. Todd, Alexander Botkin, Mr. Wheeler, Walter Lachelle, Daniel Carter, and Samuel W. Hamilton.

It is not safe to say, that every man on this list was in that mob; but that they were in sympathy with it, there can be no doubt. But in Alton, at that time, there was no chance of a conviction for taking part in a pro-slavery mob.

This trial was soon closed. Col. Alexander Botkin* was

---

* This Col. Botkin was the same who presented the resolution, so "cordially adopted," at the Market-House meeting in August, 1837. His resolution was thought, at that time, strongly to hint at mob-law, because it professed to deprecate that sort of remedy, and yet it called on Lovejoy to "cease persisting to publish an Abolition paper *to the injury of the community,*" and "to discontinue his *incendiary* publications."

Foreman of the Jury, and he promptly presented, in behalf of the rioters, a Sealed Verdict to the Court, of "Not Guilty."

Thus ended the trials at Alton, which in their day were important enough to give rise to the publication of one or two books, long since out of print.

CONCLUSION.

It hardly becomes one who has earned a place in the story, only by "allegiance to a fallen lord," to moralize on the events he has recounted.   The reader must, therefore, be left to draw his own conclusions from my facts.   To the chief actor in the drama, the occasion called for steadfast adherence to principle, and made compromise a crime. So was it with our Great Exemplar, before his final entry into Jerusalem; so was it with Martin Luther, when the gentle Melancthon justified his daring course by replying to an objector—"*The times are very sick, and need a sharp physician.*"   So has it been on innumerable occasions in the history of the world, when men who have challenged the admiration of the race, have counted life as nothing worth, compared with the importance of principle.

In 1837, the imperious beginnings of our great conflict were upon the country; the momentous events of the war have since followed, and blessed will it be for the United States, if, after another generation has passed away, the remains yet lingering of political intolerance shall have ceased throughout the length and breadth of the land.

APPENDIX.

Official Minutes of the Meeting held at Alton, November 2d, 1837—Resolutions offered by the Rev. Edward Beecher— The adjourned meeting—Resolution offered by the Attorney-General—A compromise report, with a bias—A protest and an appeal in favor of law—Mr. Lovejoy called upon to hold his peace—Alton wants "to be let alone."

At a large and respectable meeting of the citizens of the City of Alton, held at the counting-room of Messrs. John Hogan & Co., on Thursday afternoon, Nov. 2nd, 1837, Samuel G. Bailey, Esq., was called to the chair, and Wm. F. D'Wolf, appointed Secretary.*

Mr. Hogan then announced the object of the meeting to be, to take into consideration the present excited state of public sentiment in this City, growing out of the discussion of the Abolition question; and to endeavor to find some common ground, on which both parties might meet for the restoration of harmony and good-fellowship by mutual concession—expressing a fervent wish that so desirable an object might be carried into effect.

He was followed by the Rev. Edward Beecher, of Jacksonville, who stated that the proposal of such a meeting had originated from Mr. Hogan, and that it had been deemed advisable by him and by Mr. Gilman, that the fol-

* See Chapter XVI.

lowing resolutions should be laid before the meeting for their consideration:

1. *Resolved*, That the free communication of thoughts and opinions is one of the invaluable rights of man; and that every citizen may freely speak, write, and print on any subject, being responsible for the abuse of that liberty.

2. *Resolved*, That the abuse of this right is the only legal ground for restraining its use.

3. *Resolved*, That the question of abuse must be decided solely by a regular civil court, and in accordance with the law; and not by an irresponsible and unorganized portion of the community, be it great or small.

4. *Resolved*, For restraining what the law will not reach, we are to depend solely on argument and moral means, aided by the controlling influences of the spirit of God; and these means, appropriately used, furnish an ample defence against all ultimate prevalence of false principles and unhealthy excitement.

5. *Resolved*, That where discussion is free and unrestrained, and proper means are used, the triumph of the truth is certain; and that, with the triumph of truth, the return of peace is sure; but that all attempts to check or prohibit discussion will cause a daily increase of excitement, until such checks or prohibitions are removed.

6. *Resolved*, That our maintenance of these principles should be independent of all regard to persons or sentiments.

7. *Resolved*, That we are more especially called on to maintain them in case of unpopular sentiments or persons; as in no other cases will any effort to maintain them be needed.

8. *Resolved*, That these principles demand the protection of the Editor and of the press of the *Alton Observer*, on grounds of principle solely, and altogether disconnected with approbation of his sentiments, personal character, or course, as Editor of the paper.

9. *Resolved*, That on these grounds alone, and irrespective of all political, moral, or religious differences, but solely as American citizens, from a sacred regard to the great principles of civil society, to the welfare of our country, to the reputation and honor of our City, to our own dearest rights and privileges, and those of our children, we will protect the press, the property, and the Editor of the *Alton Observer*, and maintain him in the free exercise of his rights, to print and publish whatever he pleases, in obedience to the supreme laws of the land, and under the guidance and direction of the constituted civil authorities, he being responsible for the abuse of this liberty only to the laws of the land.

The meeting was then addressed at some length by Mr. Linder, in opposition to the resolutions; after which, Mr. Hayden moved that the resolutions be laid on the table. At the suggestion of Mr. Hogan and Col. Botkin, this motion was subsequently withdrawn by the mover; when Mr. Hogan moved that the resolutions be referred to a committee, with instructions to report at an adjourned meeting. This motion was agreed to; and, it being ordered that said committee should consist of seven gentlemen, to be nominated by the chair, the Hon. Cyrus Edwards, and Messrs. John Hogan, Stephen Griggs, U. F. Linder, H. G. Van Wagenen, Thos. G. Hawley, and Winthrop S. Gilman, were appointed.

Mr. Linder then offered the following resolution, which was agreed to:

Resolved, unanimously, by this meeting, That in the interim between the adjournment and reassembling hereof, if any infraction of the peace be attempted by any party or set of men in this community, we will aid to the utmost of our power in the maintenance of the laws.

The meeting then adjourned to meet at the court-room, on Friday, the 3d inst., at 2 o'clock P.M.

FRIDAY, Nov. 3d, 2 o'clock P.M.

The citizens met, pursuant to adjournment, and the meeting being called to order by the chairman, Mr. Linder offered the following resolution, which was unanimously agreed to without debate :

Resolved, That this meeting shall be composed exclusively of the citizens of Madison County; and that it is requested that none others shall vote or take part in the discussion of any subject that may be offered for their consideration; but all persons in attendance, other than citizens, will consider themselves as welcome spectators.*

The Hon. Cyrus Edwards, from the committee appointed at the previous meeting, then made the following report, which was read:

The committee appointed to take under consideration certain resolutions submitted at our last meeting, beg leave to report: that they have given to those resolutions a deliberate and candid examination, and are constrained to say that, however they may approve their general spirit, they do not consider them, as a whole, suited to the

* Mr. Beecher resides in Morgan County.   Hence the resolution.

exigency which has called together the citizens of Alton. It is notorious, that fearful excitements have grown out of collisions of sentiment between two great parties on the subject, and that these excitements have led to excesses on both sides deeply to be deplored. Too much of crimination and recrimination have been indulged. On the one hand, the Anti-Abolitionists have been charged with a heartless cruelty, a reckless disregard of the rights of man and an insidious design, under deceptive pretexts, to perpetuate the foul stain of Slavery. They have been loaded with many and most opprobrious epithets, such as pirates, man-stealers, etc., etc. On the other hand, the Abolitionists have been too indiscriminately denounced as violent disturbers of the good order of society, wilfully incendiary and disorganizing in their spirit, wickedly prompting servile insurrections, and traitorously encouraging infractions of the constitution, tending to disunion, violence, and bloodshed. These uncharitable impeachments of motives have led to an appalling crisis, demanding of every good citizen the exertion of his utmost influence to arrest all acts of violence, and to restore harmony to our once peaceful and prosperous, but now distracted, City. It is not to be disguised, that parties are now organizing and arming for a conflict, which may terminate in a train of mournful consequences. Under such circumstances have we been convened. And your committee are satisfied that nothing short of a generous forbearance, a mild spirit of conciliation, and a yielding compromise of conflicting claims, can compose the elements of discord, and restore quiet to this agitated community. They are, therefore, forced to regard the resolutions under consideration as falling short of the great end in view; as demanding too much of concession on the one side, without equivalent concession on the other. Neither party can be expected to yield everything, and to acknowledge themselves exclusively in the wrong. In this there is no compromise. There must be a mutual sacrifice of prejudices, opinions and interests, to accomplish the desired reconciliation—such a sacrifice as led to the adoption of the great charter of American freedom; which has secured to ourselves, and which promises a continuance to our posterity, of the blessed fruits of peace, prosperity, and union. Whilst, therefore, we fully and freely recognize the justness of the principles engrafted upon our constitutions, that the free communication of thoughts and opinions is one of the invaluable rights of man, and that every citizen may freely speak, write, and print on any subject, being responsible for the abuse of that liberty; that the abuse of this right is the only legal ground for restraining its use; that the question of abuse must be decided solely by a regular civil court, and in accordance with the law, and not by an irresponsible and unorganized portion of the community, be it great or small —your committee would, with earnest opportunity, urge as a means of allaying the acrimony of party strife, the unanimous adoption of the following preamble and resolutions:

WHEREAS, it is of the utmost importance that peace, harmony, order, and a due regard to law, should be restored to our distracted community; and, whereas, in all cases of conflicting opinions about rights and privileges, each party should yield something in the spirit and form of compromise: Therefore,

1. *Resolved*, That a strong confidence is entertained that our citizens will abstain from all undue excitements, discountenance every act of violence to person or property, and cherish a sacred regard for the great principles contained in our Bill of Rights.

2. *Resolved*, That it is apparent to all good citizens, that the exigencies of the place require a course of moderation in relation to the discussion of principles in themselves deemed right, and of the *highest importance;* and that it is no less a dictate of duty than expediency to adopt such a course in the present crisis.

3. *Resolved*, That so far as your committee have possessed the means of ascertaining the sense of the community, in relation to the establishment of a religious newspaper, such a course would, at a suitable time, and under the influence of judicious proprietors and editors, contribute to the cause of religion and good citizenship, and promote the prosperity of the city and country.

4. *Resolved*, That while there appears to be no disposition to prevent the liberty of free discussion, through the medium of the press or otherwise, as a general thing, it is deemed a matter indispensable to the peace and harmony of this community that the labors and influence of the late Editor of the *Observer* be no longer identified with any newspaper establishment in this City.

5. *Resolved*, That whereas it has come to the knowledge of your committee that the late Editor of the *Observer* has voluntarily proposed to the proprietors and stockholders of the *Alton Observer*, to relinquish his interest

and connection with that paper, if, in the opinion of his
friends, that course were expedient; your committee consider that such a course would highly contribute to the
peace and harmony of the place, and indicate, on the part
of the friends of the *Observer*, a disposition to do all in
their power to restore the City to its accustomed harmony
and quiet.

6. *Resolved*, That we would not be understood as reflect-
ing in the slightest degree upon the private character or
motives of the late Editor of the *Alton Observer*, by anything contained in the foregoing resolutions.

Mr. Linder then took the floor, in support and explanation of the views taken by the committee, and urged the
adoption of the resolutions reported by them, with much
earnestness. When he closed his remarks, Winthrop S.
Gilman, one of the committee, handed the following protest against some of the sentiments expressed in the
report; which he desired should be made a part of the
record of the meeting.

W. S. Gilman, from the committee, protested against so
much of the report as is contained in the resolutions; alleging it as his opinion, that the rigid enforcement of the
law would prove the only sure protection of the rights of
citizens, and the only safe remedy for similar excitements
in future.

The Rev. E. P. Lovejoy, Editor of the *Observer*, here
addressed the meeting at some length, in a speech declara-
tory of his right, under the Constitution of this State, to
print and publish his opinions, and of his determination to
stand on this right, and abide the consequences, under a
solemn sense of duty.

He was followed by Mr. Hogan, who took a wholly different view of the subject; and contended that it was the duty of Mr. Lovejoy, as a Christian and patriot, to abstain from the exercise of some of his abstract rights, under existing circumstances. In the course of his remarks, the former referred to the pledge said to have been publicly given by the latter, when he first came to Alton; and observed, that at that time he most certainly did understand Mr. L. to say, that, inasmuch as he had left a slave-holding State, and had come to reside in a free State, he did not conceive it his duty to advocate the cause of emancipation, and did not intend doing so.

The Rev. F. W. Graves then rose in explanation; and asked Mr. Hogan whether Mr. Lovejoy did not, at the time referred to, distinctly state that he yielded none of his rights to discuss any subject which he saw fit.

Mr. Hogan replying in the affirmative, Mr. G. proceeded to remark, that when Mr. L. arrived in this City, he entertained the views attributed to him by the gentleman who had just taken his seat; that a change had subsequently taken place in his opinions; and that, at a certain meeting of the friends of the *Observer*, he (Mr. L.) had made known this alteration in his sentiments, and asked advice whether it was best to come out in public on the subject; that, under the circumstances of the case, it was deemed most proper to let the paper go on—there then being no excitement in the public mind. Mr. G. next alluded to the present excited state of the popular feeling; and said that the friends of the *Observer* had lately received communications from all parts of the country, and even from Kentucky, Missouri, and Mississippi, urging the necessity of re-establishing the press.

Mr. Linder followed in reply; and said he now understood the whole matter. It was a question, whether the interest and feelings of the citizens of Alton should be consulted; or whether we were to be dictated to by foreigners, who cared nothing but for the gratification of their own inclinations, and the establishment of certain abstract principles, which no one, as a general thing, ever thought of questioning. He concluded his remarks by offering the following resolution:

Resolved, That the discussion of the doctrines of immediate Abolitionism, as they have been discussed in the columns of the *Alton Observer*, would be destructive of the peace and harmony of the citizens of Alton, and that, therefore, we cannot recommend the re-establishment of that paper, or any other of a similar character, and conducted with a like spirit.

The resolution having been read, Mr. Edwards rose, and expressed the hope that its adoption would not be pressed at this moment. He dwelt with great earnestness and effect on the importance of calmness in our deliberations; and trusted that the present meeting would be productive of good to the community. The resolution was then laid on the table.

Judge Hawley then made a few very eloquent and appropriate remarks on the subject for which this meeting had been called, and concluded by offering the following preamble and resolution, which were read, and laid on the table for the present:

WHEREAS, great and general excitement has for some

time past prevailed with the people of the City of Alton, in relation to the publication of the doctrines of Abolition, as promulgated by Mr. E. P. Lovejoy, in a paper called the *Alton Observer;* and whereas, as a consequence of that excitement, personal violence has been resorted to in the destruction of said press: Therefore,

Resolved, That whilst we decidedly disapprove of the doctrines, as put forth by the said Lovejoy, as subversive of the great principles of our Union, and of the prosperity of our young and growing City, we at the same time decidedly disapprove of all unlawful violence.

The question, on agreeing to the report of the committee, was then called for; and on motion of Mr. Hogan, the resolutions being taken up separately, were severally disposed of as follows: resolutions 1, 2, and 4, were agreed to unanimously; and resolutions 3, 5, and 6, were stricken out. The report, as amended, was then agreed to.

The resolution offered by Mr. Linder, and laid on the table, was then taken up, and agreed to; as was also that subsequently introduced by Judge Hawley, after striking out the preamble from the latter.

Mr. Krum then offered the following resolution, which was also agreed to:

Resolved, That as citizens of Alton, and the friends of order, peace, and constitutional law, we regret that persons and editors from abroad have seen proper to interest themselves so conspicuously in the discussion and agitation of a question, in which our City is made the principal theatre. The meeting then adjourned, *sine die.*

SAMUEL G. BAILEY, *Chairman.*

W. F. D'WOLF, *Secretary.*

APPENDIX B.

Contemporary discussion in the United States Senate and House of Representatives—Remarks by Clay, Calhoun, Buchanan, Henry A. Wise, Legaré, Rhett, and others—Southern members leave the hall in a body.

Extracted from the *Commercial Transcript*, Baltimore, Dec. 19, 1837.

The following extracts give the reader some faint idea of the excitement in the U. S. Congress on the subject of Slavery, forty-two years ago. Henry Clay seldom came forward without presenting in himself a specimen of moral grandeur, which excited general admiration. For many years he stood like a rock in the midst of angry waves, holding with a firm hand those great principles which alone can sustain our republic:

"The scene of those inflammatory discussions on the Abolition and Texas questions, was to-day—December 18, 1837,—shifted from the House to the Senate, producing there one of the most animated discussions ever witnessed within its walls.

A memorial from some persons in New Jersey against the annexation of Texas, presented by Mr. Wall of that State, was the first circumstance that gave rise to the exciting scenes that followed. Mr. Preston moved to have it laid on the table, and accompanied his motion with denouncing bitterly the bringing before Congress such papers, and notifying the Senate of his intention to introduce a measure, having for its object the annexation of Texas to the United States' territory. The motion to lay on the table prevailed. The sensitiveness evinced by Mr. Preston on this matter served to pitch the feelings of the other Southern Senators to a similar tone, which at once manifested itself, when Mr. Wall presented a petition from his State, praying for the Abolition of Slavery in the District of Columbia.

Mr. Grundy moved to lay it on the table. Mr. Preston having called for the question whether it should be received, a debate of deep interest took place, in which every Senator seemed to think himself bound to participate. The question resolved itself into the *right of petition*. Messrs. Clay and Davis were the most conspicuous supporters of the principle that the right of petition is invaluable, and labored to show that most of the feeling of excitement now among the people at the North upon the subject, was not so much from a support of Abolition as the result of their supposing this right to be threatened and taken from them. They thought the best plan to appease this ferment of the public mind, would be to refer the petitions to the Committee on the District of Columbia. This principle was most violently opposed by Messrs. Calhoun, Preston, Strange, Buchanan, and others, who insisted upon the gross injury to the interests of the South that would result from its being put into practice.

Mr. Preston's manner and words were especially significant. He said, the South looked to Congress for protection in such an emergency, and if that was refused, it would protect itself, for the accomplishment of which, the

proper measures would be at once resorted to.   There was
no noise or anger in the delivery of such remarks as these,
at the close of his speech, but all was solemnity and cool
earnestness.   Mr. King, of Alabama, in some exciting remarks, observed that he had been at the North recently,
and had seen how the Abolition feeling was industriously
fanned by certain political knaves and demagogues, and
was made use of for party purposes.   Mr. Davis, of Mass.,
in reply said, that if such were the case, the feeling was
confined to no particular party; and, indeed, one may see
in the Senate itself, how this question will divide the ranks
of the opposite parties there.   Mr. Clay, in reply to some
heated observations from Mr. Calhoun, upon the prospect
of disunion from the agitation of the Abolition question,
poured out one of his glowing bursts of eloquence upon
the stability of our institutions, which seemed, for a time,
to efface the subject of debate from every Senator's mind.
It was a theme on which patriots of all parties could have
but one common feeling.

Mr. Calhoun had insisted upon the absurdity of handing
over to *consideration and argument,* any petitions having
for their object such fanatical schemes as those which
characterize the Abolition memorials.   He thought they
deserved no more notice or consideration than a petition
to abolish the Christian religion, or to burn the Northern
factories.   Mr. Clay, in reply, asserted that the whole
spirit of our Government was based upon argument, and
that he held in low estimation any institutions that could
not stand such a test.   It was here he alluded, in a most
expressive manner, to a remark made to him at the com-

mencement of the late war by James Madison, who replied to some important wishes made by him, that diplo-
matic notes should cease, and action should be used—by
gravely saying, "You forget, Mr. Clay, that our Government is founded on *reason*."

The whole speech was one of the finest ever made by
the great orator.

Mr. Grundy's motion, to lay the petition on the table,
was finally carried,—25 ayes—20 nays.

The *Baltimore American* gives the following account of
the same scene:

"The debate was long, spirited, and drew forth much of
the acrimony and bitter feeling of the Senators from the
South, North, and West. The discussion began on a petition presented by Mr. Wall, of New Jersey, praying for
the Abolition of Slavery in the District of Columbia. A
motion was made to lay the petition on the table.

Mr. CLAY, of Kentucky, begged that the motion to lay
upon the table should be withdrawn; the motion was
withdrawn. Mr. Clay took the floor, and said he was
anxious to learn from the Senators representing free
States, what were the causes, and what the extent of the
Anti-Slavery feeling in the North? Was it upon the increase or upon the decrease? Was not the increase caused
by supposition, on the part of the petitioners, that the
right of petition had been invaded by a refusal on the
part of Congress to receive and refer petitions? Would
not the petitions decrease if they were referred to a committee, and a report, a calm, dispassionate, tranquil, rea-

soning report be presented for the consideration of the American People? Such was the purport of the questions presented by Mr. Clay.

Messrs. WALL, of New Jersey, PRENTISS, and SWIFT, of Vt., NILES, of Connecticut, and other Northern Senators, all responded affirmatively to the question of Mr. Clay. Without exception, they said that they believed that a reference of the petitions would limit agitation, check discussion, heal the public wounds, and, in a measure, end the getting up and reception of petitions.

The discussion branched out. Northern and Southern feeling both became enlisted, and the discussion finally seemed to rest with Mr. Clay and Mr. Calhoun. The South Carolina and Kentucky Senators both addressed the Senate three or four times, and with much warmth of feeling. Mr. Calhoun persisted in his determination against the reception of petitions, against all reference, all reports, and all discussions.

Mr. Clay as warmly persisted in favor of reception, reference, consideration, and a report from the Committee, against the prayer of the petitioners.

The Senator from South Carolina said the question of Union and Disunion hung upon the result. Mr. Clay answered that he believed no such thing. He felt convinced, he said, that the people would listen to reason, to argument, and to all dispassionate appeal, most willingly, and with universal respect. Disunion he did not fear, and he wished the Senator from South Carolina would, instead of opposing the receptions, bring in a Joint Resolution that every member of Congress should be called to order by the presiding-officer when he even made an allusion to disunion.   For himself, he would join heart and hand, in the support of such a measure.

HOUSE OF REPRESENTATIVES.

On the 20th December, 1837, the excitement in the House of Representatives, at Washington, was even greater than it had been on the 18th, in the Senate.

It then culminated in a call, by the impulsive Mr. Wise, of Virginia, for the "Southern delegation to leave the hall." They were ready then for a caucus, because, maddened by the mere presentation of humble petitions; they had not yet "screwed their courage to the sticking place," where a dissolution of the Union was to be demanded.

UNFINISHED BUSINESS was then made the order of the day in the House, and the unfinished business was well named the *further consideration of the Petitions praying for the Abolition of Slavery in the District of Columbia.*

The merit of the whole slave question was involved in the discussion, and the day has been in the House one of unusual excitement.   Mr. SLADE has had the floor the most of the day, and, coming from Vermont, where Abolitionism grows up spontaneously with children to manhood, you can imagine the character of his petitions and his speech.   To speak of it in a few words, it is the very essence of all that Thompson, Garrison, May & Co. have written and spoken on the exciting topic of Slavery.

In the very outset of his remarks he was interrupted by Mr. WISE, of Virginia, for intimating that the motion to lay Abolition memorials upon the table was the result of combination, etc., on the part of Southern members.   Mr.

Dawson, of Georgia, also called him to order for the same reference, and Mr. Slade satisfied them, by disclaiming all personal feeling, and all personal references in regard to the charge.   Mr. Slade continued his remarks, and the Southern members became more and more excited.   The Speaker at length called him to order for wandering from his subject.

Mr. LEGARE, of South Carolina, got the floor, and asked permission to say a few words.   He was under the influence of great feeling and excitement, and begged the member from Vermont not to proceed.

Mr. L., as one of the most eloquent men in the House, was too much excited at the present moment to speak with any degree of coolness.

With great ardor and gusto he vindicated the South— her dearest interests and her peace—her domestic happiness—all that she had and was—was identified with this question, and he, therefore, begged that the member from Vermont would desist.

Mr. SLADE refused again and again to yield the floor, except when called to order by the members of the House.

Mr. DAWSON, of Georgia, twice asked permission to reply to some severe remarks made by Mr. S., but Mr. S. refused to yield the floor.

Here Mr. LEGARE, much excited, moved an adjournment, although it was not then one o'clock.

Mr. Legare's motion was not in order, and of course was not put by the Speaker.   Mr. Dawson, of Georgia, called for the order of the day—the further consideration of the President's message.   The motion was not in order, and Mr. Slade was again suffered to proceed.

For a half-hour, Mr. SLADE went on without intermission, animadverting, in strong language, not merely upon Slavery in the District of Columbia, but in all the States.

Mr. DAWSON, Mr. WISE, and Mr. RHETT called him to order. But, from the nature of the subject, which I will explain by-and-bye, Mr. Slade was not out of order, and was again suffered to proceed.

The House at length became too hot, Mr. Slade's remarks too personal, and the Southern members too much excited to hear more.

Mr. RHETT and Mr. WISE, at the same moment, called him to order, and for the first time, the call ,was in order. Mr. Slade was reading the opinions of several distinguished men upon the merits of Slavery.

By a rule of the House, it is not in order to read from any document, book, or pamphlet, without the consent of the House. The members objected, and Mr. Slade was compelled to take his seat. This, however, was the least exciting part of the scene. Mr. WISE, after saying that Mr. Slade had entered into a full examination of the merits of the Slave Question, CALLED UPON THE SOUTHERN DELEGATION TO LEAVE THE HALL!! *"Agreed!"* AGREED!" AGREED!" was responded by a dozen voices, and in company with twenty or twenty-five members from the Southern States, Mr. Wise left the hall.

The House was here in great confusion. A half-dozen members rose upon the floor, calling and being called to order.

Mr. RHETT said that the Southern Delegation would

meet in the District of Columbia committee-room, at 3 o'clock.

Mr. SLADE begged permission to go on in order.

Mr. McKAY, of North Carolina, called him to order, and the Speaker told him to take his seat. His motion "to be permitted to proceed in order," was, however, put to the House, and the yeas and nays demanded. A motion was now made to adjourn. Mr. Adams, of Massachusetts, demanded the yeas and nays. The House seconded the call, and the result was 106 in favor of adjournment, and 65 against it.

Mr. CAMPBELL, of South Carolina, at this moment appeared in the Hall, having been selected by the Southern members, in the committee-room, to request the attendance of all the members representing the interests of the South.

The House then adjourned.

P.S.—Mr. SLADE'S petition for the Abolition of Slavery in the District, was accompanied with instructions to report a bill for the Abolition of Slavery in the District of Columbia.

The Report made his remarks in order, and hence the reason why he was not called to order with success.

APPENDIX C.

NOTES ON THE TEXT.

By Dr. SAMUEL WILLARD, Chicago.

AT the wish of Mr. Tanner and of the publishers, I have determined to add some further history of the times and the men herein commemorated, confirming, by the testimony of another witness, much that is here, and illustrating Mr. Tanner's statements here and there by fuller detail.

The Anti-Slavery conflict early attracted my attention and my interest; in the winter of 1830–31, I heard Wm. Lloyd Garrison lecture on slavery, to a small audience, in Julien Hall, Boston, when he was so insignificant that no opposition beset him; and though I was but a child, I learned the lesson of horror of *slavery*. My father was a personal friend of Mr. Lovejoy, and, like him, was a member of the Presbyterian church, and of that particular church in Upper-Alton to which Mr. Lovejoy used to preach. I often heard him preach, and distinctly remember his form, his face, and his manner in the pulpit and among his fellows. He was not unfrequently at my father's house. I still have, as a relic, type once used in printing the *Alton Observer*, which were thrown out when the mob of August 21st, 1837, devastated the printing-office. Several of the scenes here described were witnessed by me; and many of the actors on both sides I knew. I remember when the first copy of the *St. Louis Observer* came into our house, and I have a copy of the last issue that bore the name of the *Alton Observer*.

215

Mr. Tanner seeks to impress the reader with the fact that Mr. Lovejoy was not like Luther, and Knox, and the reformers who have been noted at once for energy and violence; and who remind us of the saying of the gospel that the kingdom of Heaven suffereth violence, and the violent take it by force. What is said on page twenty-two of his appearance and demeanor is well said. As I recall him, there comes up such a man as Mr. Tanner describes, and a round pleasant face, full of good-humor, and beaming with kindness and gentleness. I saw him in the midst of the excitement of the Convention, described on page 134, and witnessed the wonderful calmness and mildness of his demeanor when all about him were excited, and Usher F. Linder shook his fist in Mr. Lovejoy's face, so near that he lacked not much of striking him. Mr. Lovejoy was not in the least a Boanerges, or 'son of thunder,' but a *gentle* man, always. His firmness was not that of passion and obstinacy, but the gentle persistence of one who felt that he was right, and that he must prevail as the sun prevails against winter, by mild shining, and not by storm. There was no bitterness in his heart, no venom on his tongue, no sound of fury in his voice. He is entitled to be ranked with the St. John of tradition, or the sweet St. Francis di Assissi of the Catholic Church. No man seemed less fitted to stand foremost in a great struggle; and yet that dreadful lot befel him; and we see that it was best that he should be such a man, so that, to use the words of the poet, 'his virtues might plead like angels, trumpet-tongued, against the deep damnation of his taking-off.'

Mr. Tanner tells, on page 124, of the first destruction of the *Alton-Observer* press, and the destruction of the office. The office was in the second story of a building on Second Street, the principal business street of Alton; and the building was next to the Piasa Creek, which is now covered in as a sewer. Mr. Godfrey, of the firm of Godfrey & Gilman, had a considerable pecuniary interest in the office. He is reported to have disapproved of any attempt to defend the office by force, as if it were a fort; and it was reported that arms, which some of the printers had in the office, were taken away. The mob certainly took good care not to suffer any hurt. The windows were demolished by volleys of stones which were abundantly furnished by the newly-macadamized street; and after it was seen that there was no apparent resistance, a ladder was set up to a window, and one of the mob crept up. One who looked on told me that the fellow was afraid to go in, and peered into the dark room with the utmost caution, ready to make a precipitate retreat. Perhaps a little firmness then, even the swift and effective stroke of a stone, might have turned, at least for awhile, the course of events.

The noise, and the rumor of the misdeed, drew many to the spot. Among those who came was Mr. Wm. Harned, keeper of a hotel on State Street. Mr. Harned was a Kentuckian, with no liking for Abolitionists, and indeed, filled with the usual prejudices against them; but what he saw then and there changed his mind and stirred his heart, so that he joined himself to the despised band, and was with Mr. Lovejoy on the night of his death. Mr. Harned said that when he looked on, and recognized the men who, as spectators, approved the violence, such men as Caleb Stone, and Dr. Hope, and Dr. Beall, and the men whose names appear in the indictment against the rioters of November 7th, he said to himself, 'what these men hate must be good: they are never on the right side.' Thus the line began to be drawn between the true and loyal men, and the cowards and traitors to freedom and rights on the other. Mr. Harned's action forthwith corresponded to his new convictions, and he never wavered.

Mr. Tanner speaks of the rumor that armed men came from St. Louis to assist this mob (p. 129). While this may have been true, I think it was never proved that any help came to the ruffians of Alton from that source. The fast-growing towns of the West had, all of them, an abundant influx of the class of roughs; especially were the river towns so afflicted. Alton had vile men enough of her own for such deeds, especially when merchants of Second Street, doctors, and lawyers, and even such ministers of the gospel (heaven save the mark!) as John Hogan and Charles Howard either egged on the mob, or were, at best, coldly indifferent.

We are told (pp. 133, 135), that a removal of the *Observer* to Quincy was suggested. The Anti-Slavery men of that City, aided by those who determined to have law and order prevail, had a struggle with the mob-element about this very time, in which they won the victory, through the stern determination of a few men, foremost among whom was Joseph T. Holmes, afterward a Congregational minister. Once, some of the mob learned where arms of the Anti-Slavery men were stored and liable to be captured by a sudden movement; at the same time, Mr. Holmes learned that they had such knowledge; he had no time to call assistance, but went at once to the spot. He had barely reached it when some of the mob arrived. Mr. Holmes was standing on the movable plank in the floor, over the guns, with arms folded, and facing the door. Each successive mobite departed; and one of them said, narrating their failure, that "Holmes was there, and looked as if he would as soon shoot a fellow as not." The years 1836 and 1837 were the special era of mobs in the United States; and but few places were blest with a Holmes.

Mr. Tanner's fifteenth chapter relates briefly the history of the Anti-Slavery convention, held at Upper-Alton, in October. Through the medium of the *Observer* a call was

issued for the convention, signed by fifty-six gentlemen of
Quincy; forty-two of Galesburg; thirty-two of Jacksonville; twenty-three of the Altons; twenty of Springfield;
and seventy-two others in other places. There were no
signers south of Alton, and none north of Hennepin. The
call was for "a meeting of the friends of the slave and of
free-discussion." It stated that the convention should
consist of those "who believe that the system of American
slavery is sinful and ought to be immediately abandoned."
Mr. Lovejoy added a special appeal to the friends of free-
discussion and of the right of free-speech to show, by their
zeal, that they appreciated the crisis.

The Convention assembled at the Presbyterian Church,
in Upper-Alton, Thursday, October 26th, at 2 p.m., and
was called to order by Mr. Lovejoy. On his motion, Rev.
Dr. Gideon Blackburn, a venerable clergyman, was made
chairman; and Rev. F. W. Graves, of Lower-Alton, secretary. The official record says, "In consequence of the
intrusion of a number of disorderly persons, the convention
did not organize during the afternoon." This brief statement covers a curious proceeding, which I witnessed.
When the house was opened and the delegates took their
seats, along with them came Usher F. Linder, whose real
character and position are shown in the sixteenth and
seventeenth chapters, and in the appendix, page 186, Alexander Botkin, whose bloated form and face showed his
special devotions, and others of the baser sort. These
began to interrupt the meeting by noise and by making
motions on its business. Col. Botkin was the first to conceive the idea of capturing the convention by adopting the
doctrines of the call; and while the real Abolitionists were
desirous to adopt some declaration precise enough to
exclude the intruders, he insisted on adhesion to the call
and claimed that he had a right to a seat as a member.
Linder soon saw the advantage of this move, and fell in

with it; and over two hours were spent in a profitless wrangle. It was during this time that I saw Linder shake his fist, insultingly, in the face of Mr. Lovejoy, within about two feet of him. Botkin and Linder were almost constantly on their feet, jumping up at every opportunity.

After a motion to adjourn was carried, and the house was cleared, Linder, then attorney-general of Illinois, mounted a wood-pile near the church and began a furious tirade against the Yankees, meaning Northern and Eastern people, generally. He spoke of the new things they were introducing, their home-missionaries, their sunday-schools, their Abolitionism, their temperance societies,—and just at that moment he remembered that within a few days, just after a notably disgraceful fit of drunkenness, he had been induced to sign the total-abstinence pledge. Instantly correcting himself, he changed his tone and said, "But, by the way, gentlemen, temperance is a very good thing;" and for two or three minutes he made, to his rowdies, a fair temperance speech; and then he resumed his abuse of Yankees in general, Abolitionists in particular, and Mr. Lovejoy specially.

Next day, the chairman declared the call to be the basis of the organization. Immediately the Botkin party began to enroll their names. The record shows thirty-two legitimate members from Alton and vicinity, fifty-two from fourteen other counties of Illinois, and one from Wisconsin, making a total of eighty-five, some of whom were not in at first. The first vote that tested the strength of the parties was on the choice of president: seventy-three votes were cast for Dr. Blackburn, and fifty-two for Dr. Thomas M. Hope, a man who afterward, if common report was true, claimed the honor of having killed Mr. Lovejoy. And while this business was in progress, the mob-party was enrolling men as fast as possible, and drumming up recruits. In the entry of the church stood a trifling fellow, named

Arthur Jourdon, who accosted everyone who came in, thus: "Join the convention? Botkin and all our men are joining." Without a word more, names were taken; and at the third vote, on the election of the assistant-secretary, the mob had the majority, electing William Carr, the leader of the mob of November 7th. The published roll of names shows a list of one hundred and seven intruders, who thus, by falsehood, put themselves into the convention. I happen to know that the name of James H. Wilson is wrongly so enrolled, as he was an Anti-Slavery man; but not being known as such to the officers, he was supposed to be one of the mob. As I look over the roll and recall the standing of a large number of these intruders, I am even yet surprised at their joining in this trick. All of them desired to defeat the Convention; but it would have pleased them better to have it done by violence, or to look on approvingly while others did it. Among the names I see prominent politicians and officers, as Cyrus Edwards, afterward Whig candidate for governor; Rev. (!) John Hogan, I. B. Randle, O. M. Adams, George Smith, U. F. Linder, S. W. Robbins, Dr. Halderman, and others, some of whom, in later time, became Republicans in politics, and helped to overthrow slavery. The names of seven out of the ten who were indicted for the riot, ending in the death of Mr. Lovejoy, are in this list.

After the election of Mr. Carr, the convention was fully in the hands of the intruders. A communication from the Trustees of the Church, objecting to the use of the building for any one-sided discussion of the question of Slavery, played into the hands of the mob, and was loudly cheered by their side of the house.* The chair appointed a committee to report business for the convention, con-

* The Trustees were true men; but, thinking only of the benefit of free discussion, they forgot that a meeting to form a society for a specific purpose must not be a debating club.

sisting of Rev. Edward Beecher, Rev. Asa Turner, and U. F. Linder, who was quite moderate in his demeanor now. In the afternoon, these reported: Linder's resolutions were at once taken up, discussed and adopted. Did space permit, I would copy these resolutions, to show how completely foreign to the sentiment of the call they are, deprecating the immediate Abolition of Slavery, which the call approved. Nevertheless, one resolution declares "That we will use all lawful means to exterminate Slavery within the United States." It is reasonably to be doubted whether a single one of these gentlemen, many of whom I knew well, ever uttered a word against Slavery afterward, until Republican politics or the civil war opened their mouths.

The disappointed Abolitionists met next day in a private house, where no blundering trustees could control their action. While the meeting was held in Mr. Hurlbut's house, the mob-party were on hand, ready to interrupt again; but the civil authorities of Upper-Alton had met the night before and chosen good men and true to the number of forty, if I remember rightly, and sworn them in as special constables. I remember seeing one of the mob-party at a street corner, blustering and swaggering and threatening; Mr. Enoch Long and other citizens told him he mustn't behave so in that town; and he presently departed, with the air of a muzzled bull-dog.

The Anti-Slavery Society was formed with the following officers: Elihu Wolcott,* Jacksonville, *President;* Rev. Hubbell Loomis,* U. Alton, H. H. Snow,* Quincy, Thomas Powell, ———, Thomas Galt, Sangamon County, Aaron Russell,* Peoria, *Vice Presidents;* George Kimball,* Charles W. Hunter,* James Mansfield, J. S. Clark, Julius A. Willard, of the Altons, and Rufus Brown, Willard Keys,* Joseph T. Holmes, Rev. Asa Turner, Dr. Richard Eells,* Ezra Fisher, and Rev. Wm. Kirby,* of Quincy and

vicinity, *Board of Managers;* Rev. Elijah P. Lovejoy,*
Rev. T. B. Hurlbut, Maj. Chas. W. Hunter,* and Julius A.
Willard, *Executive Committee;* E. P. Lovejoy,* *Corresponding Secretary;* T. B. Hurlbut, *Recording Secretary;* P. B.
Whipple, *Treasurer;* Samuel F. Moore,* *Auditor.* Of
these, all marked * are known to be dead; "Father" Loomis
died December 15, 1872, at the age of ninety-seven and a
half years; only Julius A. Willard, my father, aged eighty-
eight, Rev. Asa Turner, of about the same age, and Rev.
Thaddeus B. Hurlbut, aged seventy-nine, are known to be
living.

The *Alton Telegraph* published the proceedings of the
mob-convention, without any narration of the facts, under
the heading "Illinois Abolition Convention."

The meeting of October 30th, (p. 136) was notable as
showing the effect of a few determined and organized men
upon the mob. As the company were going to their hall
after Mr. Beecher's sermon, they were interrupted by a
crowd of the mob; but a collision between the head of a
mobite and the breech of a gun in the hands of Moses G.
Atwood was sufficient to clear the way. Another gang
tried to waylay Mr. Lovejoy, who had to walk nearly a
mile to his home; but he had exchanged his wide-brimmed
white hat for a cap, and passed unrecognized. Then his
house was attacked; but when he appeared with a rifle in
hand, the gang fled. It was frequently thought best to
defend Mr. Lovejoy's house; a company from Upper-Alton went down several times; and more than once I saw
to it that my father's shot-gun was in order for use in this
war, with plenty of ammunition.

Mr. Tanner's chapter XVIII narrates the final catastrophe in this struggle. The fourth press was landed on the
night of November 6th, from the steamer *Missouri Fulton*,
whose captain (I wish I knew his name) had agreed to
land the press at midnight, even if he should have to lay

his boat by for a while to do so. A horn, blown by some party unknown, seemed to be signal from the mob, but none of them appeared. Mayor Krum was rather unwillingly present, a second messenger being necessary to secure the fulfillment of his promise to be present. His conduct throughout shows his imbecility, and the worthlessness of a Democratic party magistrate. Wishing to please the honest men and to do his duty, he dared not offend his constituents who were on the other side.

The picture of the building given in this volume needs some explanation and corrections. It is all out of proportion, as any one may see by comparing the ladder and the man on it, with the building. The ladder is at the north end of the building. The other or south end fronts the Mississippi River, which here flows nearly east. At the north end of the building the ground was so much higher than at the other that the buildings appeared on the north to be three stories high, but four stories high at the other end. The building nearest the spectator in the picture is on the west side; and a door, not shown in the picture, opened from the basement story on that side. The western building was about one hundred feet long, more, not less; the eastern building was a little shorter. On the north the ground rose rapidly, so that the cutting out of a narrow street on the north had left a high bank on which men could stand on a level with the second and even the third of the stories of the north end. The mob made its appearance at the south end, knocked and hailed the store. Mr. Gilman answering from the upper door, William Carr, one of the secretaries of the false Anti-Slavery convention, demanded the press, presenting a pistol at Mr. Gilman. The active attack began with volleys of stones, breaking windows on the north end, and by the firing of two guns. Messrs. Edward Keating (a lawyer) and Mr. Henry H. West (merchant and brother-in-law of John Hogan) had previously been informed by leaders of the mob of their intention to destroy the press; and these *gentlemen*, instead of busying themselves to rouse the citizens to stop the riot, became the envoys of the mob, asked to see Mr. Gilman, and were admitted to the building. Through them the mob learned that there were less than twenty men in the buildings. The forbearance of the men inside emboldened the mob. I have long been accustomed to say that it was a pity that Henry Tanner was not commander that night in place of the aged, mild, and courteous Deacon Enoch Long. The crisis required either vigorous fighting and a Napoleonic movement upon the enemy, or Quaker non-resistance. The half-way policy which was adopted produced its natural unhappy results.

The town was alarmed meantime, as much as could be: it was, and is, a scattering place, built irregularly on steep hills. Less than half a mile from the scene of action was the only church with a bell, the Presbyterian: Mrs. Graves, the wife of the pastor, herself opened the church, and little, but brave woman as she was, tolled the bell a long time; but no help was given to the besieged, or to the vacillating, impotent mayor. There was constant communication between the inside and the outside of the besieged warehouse by the envoys of the mob, the mayor himself repeatedly acting as such, and Mr. West flitting in and out to report the progress of the mob. The *Memoir of E. P. Lovejoy* says that S. W. Robbins, Justice of the Peace! was once an envoy of the mob with the mayor.

Mr. Tanner tells little of what went on inside the building. He, and some one or two others, know who fired the shot that killed Lyman Bishop; but no one tells us. Of course it was at once said that Bishop was a harmless spectator; I heard Josiah Nutter, an indicted mobite, say so; but who ever aimed at him knew what he was about; and beside, Mr. H. H. West testified in court, that those who carried Bishop off (they took him as they might have carried a hog, one by each limb) said that one of their men was hurt; and Mr. Reuben D. Farley told me that he examined the body, and found that the shot entered at the shoulder, and passed through him lengthwise, which shows that he was stooping to pick up a stone, and not standing to look on.

As these notes do not pass under Mr. Tanner's eye before the printing, I shall tell one anecdote of his action in the warehouse, which will show the coolness and courage of himself and of others in that sad strait. Mr. Reuben Gerry was in the loft of the western building, against which the ladder was afterward put; and there was stored a lot of stone-ware, jugs and jars. Mr. Gerry began to throw out upon the heads of the assaulting mob some of the stones they had thrown in through the windows, and some of the jugs and jars. There was no communication between this loft or upper story and the other, in which Mr. Tanner was posted with a rifle. Mr. Gerry's proceedings raised a yell among the mob that was trying to force the door below, and a cry arose, "Shoot that fellow!" Mr. Gerry had opened the door of his loft, and could be seen as he came forward now and then. A man went upon the bank across the street, which I mentioned above, and tried to get sight of Gerry to shoot him. Mr. Tanner immediately thrust his rifle through the sash-door of the other loft, and took aim at the fellow, determined to drop him if he seemed to get aim at Mr. Gerry. Mr. Tanner knew the man well, for it was a bright moonlight night: the same man afterward boasted that he had shot Mr. Lovejoy. Whenever he drew up to aim at Mr. Gerry, Mr. Tanner would draw sight upon him, sparing his life every time, until he gave up the attempt, because Mr. Gerry ceased his sport. The man who told me this, Mr. J. Norman Brown, said that he saw Mr. Tanner so

doing; that he had come in with Mr. H. H. West from
curiosity, and thereafter staid in to help the defenders,
and shared their risk when they went out; "for," said he
to me, "men of that sort, so considerate, but so determined, I could stand by." Mr. Tanner told me that
James Morse, Jr., and Mr. Noble, came up and saw him
so doing, but is very positive that Mr. Brown did not
come up there, and was not in the building. It seems to
me more likely that Mr. Tanner, under such circumstances,
failed to notice the stranger, or forgot him afterwards,
than that Mr. Brown, whom I knew in Upper-Alton, and
who bore a good reputation, should have told me a falsehood.

Mr. Tanner does not mention that twice a party went
out to shoot at the man on the ladder who was firing the
building. The roof did not burn readily, and as the man
was trying to kindle the fire, some four or five persons
went out at the south door, hurried to the south-west
angle of the building (miscalled in the *Memoir of Lovejoy*
the *south-east*), and fired at him. Mr. Lovejoy and Mr.
Weller were shot on their venturing out a second time, by
an ambush placed behind some lumber which was piled
on the levee. Mr. Lovejoy had strength to run into the
building, and upstairs, before he fell. Mr. Weller was
saved by Mr. Geo. H. Whitney, a druggist, my father's
partner in business, who knew how to apply a tourniquet.
How near they came to killing the man on the ladder has
never been told; but I knew a youth of some fifteen years
of age, named Okey, who had a scar over one eyebrow,
who said he received the hurt from a shot while he was
going up that ladder; but his feeling of anger was not at
the man who shot him: on the other hand, he said that if
there was another mob, he would go into it to shoot Dr.
Hope, who had persuaded him to go up the ladder.

When Mr. Lovejoy was killed, Mr. Harned insisted on

telling the mob, hoping that they would go away: he put his head out of a scuttle and told the fact in a stentorian voice, and received in reply a volley of bullets. Nutter, one of the mob, said, telling a sympathizing crowd of the night's work, "Ole Harned stuck out his head and told us that Lovejoy was dead." But the mob was now blood-thirsty. Mr. Roff determined to go out and secure terms of surrender; as soon as he put one foot out of doors he was wounded in the ankle. Finally, Mr. West came to the north door and urged the defenders to surrender the press: if they would do so, the "boys" would put out the fire, and allow them to go unhurt. The arms being secreted, the defenders left the house, but were fired upon at once by the mob, whose bullets, fired from higher ground, passed harmlessly over them. They ran for life till pursuit ceased. It was at this time, I think, that a man, pursuing Mr. Tanner, fired at him on State Street, finding that Mr. Tanner was out-running him: the bullet cut Mr. Tanner's coat on one shoulder. He told my father that he never knew before why the Lord made him so short: if he had been larger, he would have been killed. As to the fire on the roof of the warehouse, none of the mob were ready to keep their promise to put it out when the house was surrendered; I heard that Mr. West had to put it out with his own hands.

When Mr. Lovejoy's corpse was taken home in the morning, Dr. Beall, who subsequently perished in a brawl in Texas, seeing it borne by, said, "If I only had a fife, I'd play the Dead March for him."

Mr. Tanner gives on page 166, in a foot-note, the names of the defenders of the warehouse: had the assault been foreseen, not twenty, but fifty or sixty names would have been in the roll. I took much pains at the time to make up a list, and long supposed that I had the only one in existence. I conversed with several who were there, and

asked them to correct my roll.   I had the impression that
I talked with Mr. Tanner himself, as I certainly did with
Mr. Enoch Long, Mr. Geo. H. Whitney, Mr. Hurlbut, Mr.
Samuel J. Thompson, Mr. Edward Breath, and Mr. Reuben D. Farley.   My list differed from Mr. Tanner's in two
or three particulars.   I left out the name of George T.
Brown, for he left the building early in the night and
could not return: he was a young man then about sixteen
or seventeen years old.   I had not the name of Mr. J. C.
Woods, who was not known to me; he was a blacksmith,
and died about 1851, at Alton.   Mr. H. D. Davis is unknown to me.   My list, therefore, did not include these.
It includes two others not named by Mr. Tanner, *viz.:* Mr.
Mr. Reuben D. Farley, now living in Jerseyville, Ill., who
talked with me about his being there, in the presence of
Mr. Whitney, who was there.   And next, Mr. J. Norman
Brown, who was not in originally, but chose to stay, as I
have told above.   I am sure that both these persons were
there as they told me: Mr. Tanner is sure they were not
there: in my mind, the testimony of those who saw them
prevails over his who did not.

Mr. Royal Weller afterward married the widow of Mr.
Lovejoy.   Toward the close of his life he was for a time
insane, but recovered.   When Dr. Thomas M. Hope, afterward Democratic candidate for Congress, came in with the
mob, he wanted to extract the ball from Mr. Weller's leg;
but he said he would rather die than have help from one
of the murderous mob.   Mr. Amos B. Roff, a stove-dealer,
removed to St. Louis.   Mr. Harned left Alton and went
upon a farm, where he died.   Mr. Reuben Gerry and Mr.
George H. Walworth were partners as Gerry & Walworth.
Mr. James Morse died in 1865.   Mr. Edward Breath was
a printer, (as mentioned in the note to page 15), and died
in Syria or Persia, as a missionary.   Mr. Whitney was of
the firm of Willard & Whitney: he received a ball that

night in his clothing, of which he was ignorant at the time. Mr. Noble was of the firm of Van Antwerp & Noble. Five, Messrs. Long, Thompson, Hurlbut, Loomis, and Brown, were from Upper-Alton. Mr. Long, a much-esteemed citizen, must be over ninety years of age, by this time: he then seemed to me past middle age. Mr. Sam'l J. Thompson chose not to leave the building with the others, and, while intending to be out of the way, wandered into the room where the box containing the press was, and sat down upon it. When the ruffians offered to throw him out of the upper door, he answered they could do it, but whoever should try it would go with him. He was very strong and as active as a cat, and would have made good his promise. He afterward went to Mobile, Ala., and soon died there, I think in 1840. I knew his widow. Rev. Mr. Hurlbut still lives at Upper-Alton; a year ago, when he was at the advanced age of seventy-eight, he was so brave as to undergo an operation for cataract. Mr. David Burt Loomis, son of the Rev. Hubbell Loomis, mentioned above, was a salesman in the store of Godfrey & Gilman, and used his gun, loaded with buckshot, again and again. Mr. Daniel F. Randle was a clerk in the house of Flagg & North. Mr. Reuben D. Farley was, like Thompson and J. Norman Brown, a carpenter, and afterward studied and practised medicine. Messrs. Tanner and Gilman speak for themselves in these pages: both are still active, busy, and useful men.

I attended the first part of the trial of the twelve who were indicted as stated on page 188. I remember how a certain J. S. McFarland, who was as notorious a mobite as Dr. Hope himself, tried to get on the jury, stepping into the bailiff's way when he had to summon talesmen. He professed to have no opinion or prejudice in the case, but was peremptorily challenged. Usher F. Linder fairly pushed himself into the prosecution, though Mr. F. B.

Murdock, the city attorney, said he had no occasion for his help, and was manifestly unwilling to be joined with him.   The whole proceeding was so manifestly a farce that some of the parties indicted never received any notice of the proceeding against them.   The fact was, that the pro-slavery part of the grand jury would find no indictment against Carr, Hope, and that gang, unless the other members would agree in finding the absurd one against Mr. Gilman and other defenders.

It is not known who fired the fatal shot or shots that slew Mr. Lovejoy.   Dr. Hope and Dr. Beall were equally ready to boast of it.   It was believed by many that James M. Rock, a drayman, who subsequently was sentenced for some violent crime to the Ohio State Penitentiary, fired the shot.   It soon ceased to a matter of boasting, as the contempt and hatred of mankind began to tell upon those who had tried to slay the right of free-speech.   The wide-spread and deep indignation that stirred myriads of hearts throughout the land did more to drive nails into the coffin of Slavery than Mr. Lovejoy could have done in a long life.   This was the battle of Concord in the great Anti-Slavery Revolutionary War.   From that day, the mob-spirit waned, and slavery lost contest after contest, till the mighty North sent its armies to slay Treason and Slavery and give them a common grave.

Mr. Tanner has not mentioned the effect which this summer of violence and autumn of murder had upon the fortunes of the City of Alton.   With certain advantages of position, and with the superiority that should naturally belong to a city in a free-state, it was trying to rival the much older City of St. Louis.   The panic and commercial failures of 1837 struck it a hard blow; but the "Lovejoy Riots" dealt it a well-nigh fatal one.   Its righteous men, its sixty brave defenders of the right were forgotten, when men thought of Hogan and Howard and Hope, of Beall and Carr and Linder. The warehouses that had been built in its youth of enterprise were soon deserted and sold for tenths or twentieths of their cost. Many of the Anti-Slavery men moved away. A store which Mr. Tanner had built at a cost of over $25,000, and sold for less than half that sum, was offered him again for $2000.

The following extracts, from newspapers of the time, were unjustly severe, there is no doubt; but they serve to show what was then thought and said of Alton, and how the riots, told of in this book, helped to sink it and destroy the hopes of its better citizens, who struggled vainly against such ill fame:

"The theatre of murders, of bloody and outrageous deeds of infamy has been transferred from Vicksburg to Alton. Let this place be forever remembered—let its name be written in the catalogue of all that is exécrable— let the emigrant avoid it as he values his liberty—let him pass by on the other side of this Sodom of the West, lest if he should tarry in it, the wrath of insulted heaven in fire and water should descend and destroy the place with its wicked, pusillanimous and shameless inhabitants, who, like base cowards, permitted the murder of one of their fellow-citizens. There can be no excuse offered on their part."— *Caledonian, Vt.*

"What freeman—who but a savage, or cold-hearted murderer would now go to Alton? Meanness, infamy, and guilt are attached to the very name. Hereafter, when a criminal is considered too base for any known punishment, it will be said of him—'he ought to be banished to Alton,' or, 'he ought to be banished to a place as *vile and infamous as Alton*'—a place where freedom is disowned— where the *defenders* of freedom are murdered by the consent of the inhabitants—where the inhabitants themselves are *land-pirates*—where the Attorney-General, the representative of the State, instead of bringing criminals to judgment, *encourages, spurs them on*, to the perpetration of the foulest crimes, the basest murder; and the Mayor of the City sits as a judge-advocate for the mob."—*Lynn Record, Mass.*

I disinter these fragments as a part of the history of the time, to show the obloquy that was poured out upon the City of Alton, and especially upon Linder and Krum. Mild men spoke less violently, but with as stern a reprobation. So long as that generation survived, the reputation of Alton could not be redeemed. While the cowardly men, and the violent men overpowered the better class, there was no hope for it. The *Alton Telegraph*, the leading paper, dared say nothing for freedom or right. Six years after Lovejoy's death, some of the same fellows of the baser sort, seized a colored woman, whose right to freedom was about to be contested in the courts, and carried her over into Missouri, in a frail boat, making way among the floating winter ice, at the risk of their lives; I doubt whether any of the better people of Alton knew anything of it, even after it was done.

But when the decisive struggle of the civil war came, the sons of those who had persecuted the prophets a quarter of a century before, took their places in the ranks to fight and die for liberty; and Alton sent her quota to sustain the grand cause for which Lovejoy had died: and of him, as of a later enemy of Slavery it might well be said—

HIS SOUL IS MARCHING ON!

Chicago, Dec. 25th, 1880.